MIND LAUNDRY

SMARTEN UP THE WAY YOU THINK, ACHIEVE THE GOALS YOU WANT

GERRY KUSHEL

Viva Books Private Limited
New Delhi • Mumbai • Chennai • Kolkata • Bangalore • Hyderabad • Kochi

First Indian Edition 2007

VIVA BOOKS PRIVATE LIMITED

- 4737/23 Ansari Road, Daryaganj, New Delhi 110 002
E-mail: vivadelhi@vivagroupindia.net, Tel. 42242200
- Plot No. 76, Service Industries, Shirvane, Sector 1, Nerul, Navi Mumbai 400 706
E-mail: vivamumbai@vivagroupindia.net, Tel. 27721273, 27721274
- Jamals Fazal Chambers, 26 Greams Road, Chennai 600 006
E-mail: vivachennai@vivagroupindia.net, Tel. 28290304, 28294241
- B-103, Jindal Towers, 21/1A/3 Darga Road, Kolkata 700 017
E-mail: vivakolkata@vivagroupindia.net, Tel. 22836381, 22816713
- 7, Sovereign Park Apartments, 56-58, K. R. Road, Basavanagudi, Bangalore 560 004
E-mail: vivabangalore@vivagroupindia.net, Tel. 26607409, 26607410
- 101-102 Mughal Marc Apartments, 3-4-637 to 641, Narayanguda, Hyderabad 500 029
E-mail: vivahyderabad@vivagroupindia.net, Tel. 27564481, 27564482
- Bee Vee Towers, First Floor, SRM Road, Kaloor, Kochi - 682 018, Kerala
E-mail: vivakochi@vivagroupindia.net

Published by arrangement with

Thorogood Publishers Limited
10-12 Rivington Street
London EC2A 3DU,
UK

ISBN 81-309-0380-6

Published by Vinod Vasishtha for Viva Books Private Limited, 4737/23, Ansari Road, Daryaganj, New Delhi 110 002.

Printed by Sanat Printers, Kundli - 131028.

This book is dedicated with great love and affection to all my family members and especially to our grandson Alexander Raymond Davis.

Dr Gerald Kushel

Contents

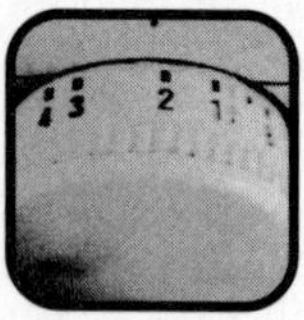

Introduction

In this Mind Laundry book, I want to help you to smarten up the way you think to achieve the goals you want at work and in your personal life. I will put your mind through these four programme cycles:

Programme 1:	'Relentlessly aim to have a full and satisfying life'
Programme 2:	'Proactively choose thoughts that provide you with a full and satisfying life, but not at the expense of others'
Programme 3:	'Periodically assess your managerial strengths and weaknesses'
Programme 4:	'Systematically improve bit by bit'

You will then be cleansed of those elements that prevent effective thinking and you will emerge from the MIND LAUNDRY able to improve the way you think and act at all times, and be able to achieve life and work satisfaction and success.

We as individuals know that we should strive to take pride in our personal appearance and there are industries and the media to tell us what to wear and what not to wear and help us improve our personal grooming. For clothes we have the laundry and the dry cleaners.

We as individuals are encouraged to take a pride in our surroundings – where we live, the way we live and how we can redesign our houses and gardens: even to put ourselves through a life laundry or address home cleanliness.

We as individuals are shown how to improve the way we cook and what we eat.

We as individuals are encouraged to take physical exercise and improve the condition of our bodies.

But, this book concentrates on how to improve the way we think – how to put ourselves through a MIND LAUNDRY to smarten up the way we think to achieve the goals we want.

The power that runs my Mind Laundry is Effective Thinking. I will show you, step by step, how to use effective thinking, both inwardly and outwardly.

Effective thinkers always take full responsibility for their own thoughts, their own feelings and, of course, their own behaviour. They never seriously blame any other person, place or thing for what they do, think or feel. Moreover, they are down to earth and realistic. They face life directly, rapidly overcome any hardships or setbacks that come their way and get on with making their lives as rich and as satisfying as is humanly possible.

Effective thinkers do all they can to change those things that they can – they develop the wisdom to know the difference between what can be changed and what cannot be changed.

Effective thinkers learn to understand their own minds, to know how to respond mentally to situations and then are better placed to understand other people and relate better with them.

Once you learn how to use effective thinking to understand your own mind, and understand others, you will want to sustain that success. The Mind Laundry Test Programme in the Appendix will keep you on track and you should come back to it periodically in the future – revisit the Mind Laundry to keep your thinking smart and effective.

Dr Gerald Kushel

PART ONE

GETTING YOUR MIND TO WORK FOR YOU

Overview

Getting your mind to work for you is achieved by gaining expertise in a process I call effective thinking. The very first step in becoming an effective thinker is to aim for a full and satisfying life, but not at the expense of any other person. The second and **final** step is to proactively, consistently do the kind of thinking (effective thinking) that will almost certainly create that full and satisfying life for you, and not at the expense of any other person. You open the door to getting your mind to work for you with two Mind Laundry 'programmes'.

The programmes in the Mind Laundry that open the door to give you the control over your own mind

PROGRAMME 1

Relentlessly aim for a 'full and satisfying life, but not at the expense of any other person.'

PROGRAMME 2

Proactively choose the kind of thoughts (effective thoughts) that provide you with the 'full and satisfying life' that you seek.

These two programmes, used in sequence, are all that you will ever need to successfully get your mind to work for you – *no matter how difficult things are or become.*

The word 'effective' means getting the result you want. Consequently, the definition of an effective thought is – *'any thought whatsoever that leads directly or indirectly toward the result you want.'* In the case of effective thinkers, the result that they want is – *the achievement of a very full and satisfying life, but not at the expense of any other person.*

The effective thinking system has deep roots

'Effective thinking' is a term that I use to describe a *system of thinking* that is backed by a great many years of research and a long history. It can be traced to early Grecian philosophy. For example, it was the ancient philosopher Epictetus (AD 60 to 117) who expressed the opinion that 'only very foolish persons become overly upset about setbacks and other things over which they have no control.'

Effective thinking is also rooted in psychology (the work of Beck, Ellis, Perls, Rogers and others). It can also be found in theology. There are many effective thoughts that can be found in **all** of the major religions. And it is supported by recent studies in neurological science and medical (brain) research. When all this is mixed with down-to-earth, practical, common sense it becomes the *Effective Thinking Process.*

My main contribution (I've been told) is the development of the above wisdom into *an uncomplicated and clear system that busy people can readily use.*

(Please note that while the substance of the real-life cases and examples that I give is authentic, all of the actual names and identifying data are fictional, to protect the confidences that effective thinkers and others shared with me).

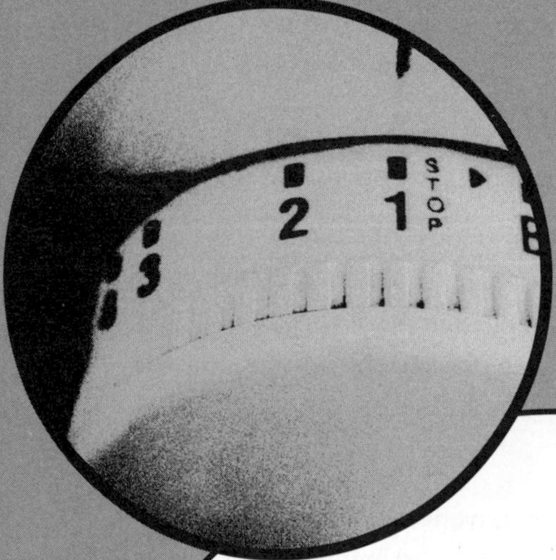

PROGRAMME ONE

'Relentlessly aim to have a full and satisfying life.'

Chapter one explains why this is the essential first step toward understanding yourself and getting your mind to work for you.

ONE
The meaning of 'full' and 'satisfying'

The first step in becoming an effective thinker and, hence, understanding and using your mind in a better way is to commit yourself toward the passionate pursuit of 'a full and satisfying life, but not at the expense of any other person.' Let me explain exactly what I mean by 'a full and satisfying life.'

The meaning of 'full'

By full, I mean *psychologically* 'rich,' not necessarily *materially* 'rich'. One can be a material multi-millionaire, and at the same time be a psychological pauper.

FENTON'S WORRIES

Fenton owned a huge, gorgeous mansion just outside of the city. He also owned a marvellous town house in London. In addition, he was the head of a thriving business. In fact, Fenton possessed just about every material luxury you could think of. He had all that money could buy – expensive cars, world travel, a busy social calendar. But still, with all this, he seemed to be in a constant state of worry. Moreover, even with all that he had, he was still extremely jealous of anyone who seemed to be doing the slightest bit better than he was. He worried about keeping his many possessions. He worried about making even more money. He worried about his children, day and night. He was insanely jealous of his beautiful new girlfriend. All this led Fenton to a series of anxiety attacks.

Clearly, Fenton was a **material multi-millionaire**, but he was also a **psychological pauper**.

Yet there are others who are quite the opposite. Psychological multi-millionaires, but who have relatively little material success.

PATRICIA'S PLEASURES

Patricia barely made a living running her small bookstore. But she loved her life. She enjoyed her work. She adored good books. And she especially took great pleasure in speaking with those that came into her shop to browse, even if they didn't buy anything. Patricia had only two wonderful friends. Every day brought her great joy.

Patricia was a psychological millionaire but a material pauper.

Some special persons are fortunate enough to be both **psychological** and **material millionaires**.

KEITH, A DOUBLE WINNER

Keith loved his work as head of a successful corporation. He was good at his work and the large amount of money that he made from it didn't hurt either. One of his passions was the 'hands on' building of a holiday home in the country. He loved working on this project in his spare time. It not only gave him great pleasure, but his wife and children enjoyed helping him to work on it as well. His life was filled with love (a close family, wonderful children, good relationships on the job, and a few good friends). When things in life got tough, as they sometimes did, Keith was able to handle difficulties with relative ease. He could deal with setbacks and success with equal aplomb. He looked upon life as a wonderful adventure. It was clear that Keith was, both materially and psychologically, very wealthy.

If, somehow, you are ever given a choice between being *only* a psychological millionaire or *only* a material multi-millionaire, it makes sense to take psychological riches as your first choice. By using effective thinking, you will able to actually guarantee that you will always be psychologically 'rich.' But since material riches depend on serendipitous forces outside of yourself, good luck is required. Being in the right place at the right time. With effective thinking, you, to a great extent, will be able to make your own luck.

Warning: don't chase happiness

It is important to make a clear distinction between 'satisfaction' and 'happiness.' One can be drugged or drunk and be 'happy.' But generally that kind of happiness is empty. Not really very 'satisfying.' 'Satisfaction' is a richer, deeper quality. The lives of Churchill, Curie, Einstein, Lincoln, Moses, Van Gogh and Michelangelo were said not to be very happy ones, but, for them, it would have been quite satisfying if they somehow could sense that someday posterity would value their unique contributions.

Certainly a sensitive and fully conscious person cannot be deeply 'happy' knowing that two thirds of the people in this world will be going to bed hungry tonight. Can you be truly happy if you know that an innocent child is being abused right now? That some really decent person, right at this very moment, is being treated very badly? That untreated cancers and heart attacks and other brutal diseases are taking life after life?

Deep 'satisfaction,' can sometimes be had simply by making a condolence call on someone who has lost a loved one. That certainly would not be a very happy experience, but it could be a satisfying one. It can be satisfying to work long and hard at a project you believe in, even if you did not have a particularly happy time working on it.

Interestingly, 'happiness,' as delightful a state as it may be, is best achieved by deliberately not chasing after it. Satisfaction, as I will be explaining, can definitely be achieved in the chase. You will do much better in your life if you consider happiness to be an occasional by-product in your life, rather than as a goal to chase or pursue.

Chasing happiness is like chasing an elusive butterfly

Chase after a butterfly and often you will chase it away. But concentrate on the flowers in the garden and sometimes that butterfly will land on your shoulder.

You can successfully chase 'satisfaction'

For effective thinkers, it is in the **pursuit, the chase**, for genuine satisfaction that provides them with zest and pleasure. The chase is a worthy one. And when they achieve satisfaction, as they do from time to time, they quickly set their sights at another (perhaps even higher) level of life satisfaction. In fact, they love the chase, even more than the actual achievement.

I conducted a survey asking a variety of persons:

'What is it that gives you genuinely most satisfaction in your life?'

There were three ingredients that appeared consistently, time and again. The three ingredients of life satisfaction are:

1. Plenty of inner calm;
2. A sense of passionate purpose; and
3. Lots of fun and adventure.

These three ingredients are all that are needed to provide a rich and satisfying life for you, but not at the expense of others. All effective thinkers strive for these three ingredients consistently: inner calm, passionate purpose and adventure. Let's explore each of these in turn.

1 Plenty of inner calm

It doesn't take much imagination to realise that you could not have a very full and satisfying life if you were nervous most of the time. As a therapist, I've been exposed to many executives who looked calm on the surface, but underneath, they were racing nervously, a mile a minute. Beneath their seemingly calm exteriors, they were nervous wrecks. Later in this book, I'll be explaining to you how you will be able to have all the inner calm you could possibly want by using effective thinking to your advantage.

However, effective thinkers explain that, it isn't enough to have nothing but inner peace: life with only inner peace can become extremely boring after a while. You also need a passionate purpose.

2 A passionate purpose

Effective thinkers have a sense of passionate purpose. How about adding some passion of purpose to your life, if you have been neglecting that aspect of life lately? Have you clarified for yourself, your own special life mission? After all, when you were born, the mould was broken and thrown away. There never was a person exactly like you in the history of the world, and when you go there will never be another person exactly like you again. You have a special and unique purpose. Have you clarified that purpose for yourself? If not, in due course, I will be showing you how to clarify that, too.

3 Plenty of fun and adventure

Effective thinkers say, 'It is only partially satisfying to have plenty of inner calm and a passionate purpose, but I also want a little fun and adventure too.'

Even if you were to have plenty of inner calm and a passionate purpose, you would still need a bit of fun and adventure. Having adventure requires that you take some risks. I will be explaining how to have that, too.

Calm, purpose and adventure are universals

These three elements of a satisfying life are not capricious. Calm, purpose and adventure tie-in with both the largest and smallest aspects of the universe. Let's examine the big picture first.

The big (macro-scopic) picture

If the earth could speak and you were to ask her about her 'inner calm' – she would say – 'I'm grounded. I spin around and create gravity. That's my inner calm.' Then ask her about her 'purpose' and she would say, 'That's easy, my purpose is to go around the sun each and every year of my life.' And what then, you might ask, do you do for fun and 'adventure?' And she would say, 'I've got this loony moon spinning around me causing tides, and strange events. This moon of mine makes my trip around the sun each year a lot of fun and I have some real surprises as I move along on my annual journey.'

The small picture

Calm, purpose and adventure are also micro-cosmic. Nuclear physicists explain that the neutrons, electrons and protons that compose the microscopic atom have exactly the same arrangement as the sun, the moon and the earth. It makes sense, doesn't it, that one would need all three ingredients in order to be in harmony with the large and the small of the universe. Instead of making life difficult, make it easy for yourself, by not trying to swim upstream. Enjoy being carried and supported by the natural flow of the universe. The calmer you get, the easier it will be for you to clarify your passionate purpose. And the calmer you are and the clearer you are about your purpose, the easier it will be to take sensible risks, to have more fun and adventure. All this adds up to your having a richer, fuller and more satisfying life.

Never at the expense of any other person

Is it really possible for one to attain life satisfaction, as stated, but *not at the expense of any other person*? The answer is 'yes.' Of course to do that is not always easy, but effective thinkers do it. They know how. The full and satisfying life that they so passionately seek requires absolutely nothing from anyone else. It is all achieved through attitude. Since an attitude (or thought) comes free of charge, not at the expense of anyone (other than the person doing the thinking) – no one else ever need suffer if the effective thinker is enjoying his or her life.

All this, I assure you, will become clearer and clearer as we go along.

The pursuit of life satisfaction is urgent

Effective thinkers know that they are definitely not going to live forever, and, of course, no one will, not even you. The answer to the question of what it is that you aim to achieve out of this life of yours is urgent. Once you are clear that you very much want to have a full and satisfying life, then that pursuit should be the number one priority on your agenda, every day.

You are on 'vacation from eternity'

Your three score and ten or even four or five score years are not very much when you compare them with the time that you will be dead (for eternity). So then isn't it reasonable to look upon your lifetime as just 'a very short vacation' away from the billions of years that you will be in so-called eternity?

I have learned to look at my life exactly that way, and such a view has served me in very good stead. And with such an outlook, a 'vacation' mentality, I do as much as I can to make the most of it, and conversely, as *little* as I can to spoil it.

A number of years ago, in the midst of a very cold winter, I went on a week's vacation with my family to Central America. The sun was shining down there, and it was just beautiful being alive. Yet, on the second day out, the bus that was scheduled to take us on a tour was very late. Some of our fellow vacationers carried on as if their lives were coming to an end. They ranted and raved, complaining bitterly to the tour guide, who had little or no power to remedy the unfortunate circumstances. I voiced a firm complaint also, assuming that it might do some good, but I refused to get myself *internally* upset. After all, I was on vacation, and I was just delighted to be away from the cold winter for a few days. Nothing, I had determined in advance, could possibly spoil my vacation. And nothing did. Not the late tour bus, the angry passengers, or anything else. It turned out to be a marvellous trip because I was determined in advance to make it that way and knew from the start that I would.

I have exactly the same attitude now towards my entire life.

> **Don't spoil your short vacation from eternity**
>
> Nothing or no one is going to spoil my short vacation from eternity, if I have anything to do with it – and of course I have a great deal to do with it.

Naturally, opportunist that I am, if there is another life offered to me in the hereafter, I will be glad to accept it, but as for now, well this life is the 'bird in the hand.' No waiting for retirement for me, before I begin enjoying myself. Today. This is it. You, too, are on your short vacation and can decide in advance, with determination, that you are going to enjoy it, that you're going to have as satisfying a life as possible.

Of course, I am not advocating dropping everything and just going out and doing anything that comes to mind. That may bring you infantile, immediate gratification, but not much of lasting significance. Effective thinkers attempt to experience qualitatively and in depth the best that any human being is capable of experiencing, in terms of such qualities as 'love,' 'excitement,' 'purpose,' and 'feeling.'

The emphasis is firmly biased toward quality rather than quantity. A life of empty hedonism and 'more, only more' is insufficient for effective thinkers. Although they do not expect to do everything, they do expect a life in which they are able to share with and come close to others, to deal with what life has to offer head on, with vitality and enthusiasm. They do not seek to escape from this, the only life they can be sure of, by sitting it out or watching from the sidelines. They prefer active engagement in life. They take risks in business – sometimes failing – but always with the will to pick themselves up and become involved again, more intelligently perhaps, but involved nonetheless.

The crucial question about satisfaction is, 'What do you seek?' What is it that you, personally, desire out of this finite life of yours? If you are genuinely committed to having a full and satisfying life, but not at the expense of any other person, you will most certainly be able to achieve it. In the next chapter, I will help you make that commitment.

TWO

Making the commitment

In order to deepen your commitment to having a full and satisfying life, but not at the expense of any other person, here are nine life-goal, clarifying exercises. Each one of these exercises is designed to help you to clarify for yourself what it is that you want from this one and only life of yours.

Exercise 1: Your five year plan

How old will you be five years from now? Put in writing how old you will be five years from now. Seeing your age in writing will bring the possibility closer to you.

My age five years from now ______________.

What three things do you hope to accomplish over the next five years? Write them down below:

1 ____

2 ____

3 ____

Discussion

By listing your age and three things you hope to accomplish over the next five years, you will have a picture in front of you of some things that are important to you. Look them over and put the three things in priority order, 1, 2 and 3.

Exercise 2: Things you hope to achieve before your life is over

With a little luck, you'll be around for more than five years. Maybe a very long time. In any case, consider now what you hope to achieve before your life ends. Finish the open ended sentence stem, each time a bit differently.

One thing I want to do before my life is over is:

____

____

Another thing I want to do before my life is over:

____

____

Another thing I want to do before my life is over:

____

____

Another thing I want to do before my life is over:

____

____

Discussion

Look at what you have written. Was it exactly the same as in exercise one, or was it a bit different? Did you add anything? Consider why, if you did, and whether it is important enough to do in the next five years or so. Why or why not?

Exercise 3: Bad news from the doctor

Imagine that you have just left your doctor's office. He has obtained for you a third consultant's opinion and the doctor has just informed you that you will definitely have, at best, only one year left to live. He said, 'I am very, very sorry. I have checked and double-checked all the x-rays and medical reports and I am truly sorry, but based on the best medical evidence we have, it is absolutely certain, that 365 days from now – you will no longer be with us. You will no longer be alive. You will not be in any pain. You will not be suffering, but you have only 365 days left.' After leaving the doctor's office, and assuming that you have full confidence in his report, what three things would you be sure to do, in the next 365 days?

List them below, in priority order.

Three things that I would be sure to do in the next 365 days if I knew for certain that I had only one year left to live:

1 ____

2 ____

3 ____

continued over

Then take this exercise a step forward. Assume that 11 months have passed and you have procrastinated on the above (denial, even in the face of overwhelming evidence is not uncommon). Your doctor now informs you that for sure, you have only 30 days left to live. Now, what three things would you do?

1____

2____

3____

The next phase. You find that you now have only 48 hours left to live. Is there anything different that you would do, if that is all the time that you had left? List the three things that you would do (in your own shorthand) below:

1____

2____

3____

Discussion

I have asked many participants to complete this exercise as part of various training seminars. Most people list 'getting my affairs in order,' 'travel,' and 'getting together and sharing with my loved ones,' as some of the more important things that they would be sure to do.

When are you going to begin doing these things that are so important to you?

You know, of course, that a time will definitely come when you do have only very little time left. Isn't it better that you start right away to do some of these things that are important to you, rather than put them off until later?

Exercise 4: Your epitaph

Imagine that you are taking a walk on a beautiful green grassy knoll. The sky is a bright blue and there are many white fleecy clouds. You are feeling very good. The air is fresh. Things are going well. It is a very beautiful day. Then off to your right, you spot a white object at the edge of the horizon. You walk over to it and as you get closer to it you realise that it is a marble tombstone. When you reach it, you lean closer and read the inscription on it. It says, much to your astonishment, 'Here lies (your name).' And then under your name is an epitaph.

Pause and reflect for a moment. The time will surely come when someday you will pass away. If you, just now, could create for yourself a fitting epitaph that described what you really wanted out of your life, what would that epitaph be?

In your own shorthand, indicate below how you would like to be remembered.

____

____

____

____

Now, write your epitaph below:

HERE LIES ______________________________ (YOUR NAME)

____

____

____

____

Discussion

Of course, the good news is that you are not dead yet. If you are not doing very much these days to live up to your epitaph, it's time now to move into action. For example, if you had as your epitaph, 'a loving and devoted husband/wife' that can serve to remind you that family is very important to you. Then, you may see more clearly that one of your goals is to be a more loving and devoted husband/wife. Some people put as their epitaph – 'he/she tried.' What does that suggest? To me, it seems that a person with that as an epitaph wants to do the best possible with the time they have remaining. Effective thinkers had epitaphs such as 'he/she cared.' Or 'he/she really had a great life.' Effective thinkers, as you might have expected, had a clear desire to give the most and get the most and make their lives as vital as humanly possible. Do you see such an implication in the epitaph you designed for yourself? If so, you're clearly on the right track.

Exercise 5: One hour, one person

If you knew for sure that you had but one hour left in your life, what one person would you choose to spend that last hour with? Please, only one person, not two or three.

Write that person's name or initials below:

____

Discussion

This exercise can help you sort out in your own mind who is really important to you and why. Many people can more easily list two or more individuals. Listing only one requires that you sort out your values about significant people in your life.

Exercise 6: I'm sorry that...

This exercise, as with the one preceding, requires good use of your imagination. Imagine that it is ten years later than it is right now. You are ten years older. Shut your eyes and visualise yourself as an older person. Then open your eyes, pretending that it is **really** ten years later. You are older. Prices are higher. You and all your colleagues, friends and family members are older, but for the sake of this exercise, nothing else has really changed in your life and that over the past ten years, your life has been, more or less, at a standstill. You never did all of those exciting things that you intended to do. (Pretend that your career has remained at a standstill, that book you hoped to write was never written, that degree you hoped to receive was never earned, that money you hoped to make, wasn't, etc, etc).

Then after you run through in your mind all of the things that you **didn't** do, that you wish that you had done – stop. Now complete each of the following:

I'm sorry that I never (over the past 10 years)

____

____

____

____

continued over

I'm sorry that I never

I'm sorry that I never

I'm sorry that I never

I'm sorry that I never

Discussion

Of course, it is not really 'ten years later.' It still is 'now.' You may actually have many more years ahead of you, who knows for sure. If so, then you most certainly can accomplish many of the things that you listed. But again, ask yourself: am I actively moving toward the accomplishment of the things that I have put on my list of 'I'm sorry thats?' If you are, that is excellent. And if you are not, isn't it about time for you to begin? What are you waiting for? Most people are not sorry for the things that they did do, but for the things that they didn't do. The road to achievement begins with that first step. Looking ahead, it usually seems that we have all kinds of time. Looking backwards, time seems to go very fast. It does not pay to put off doing the really important things in your life.

Exercise 7: Urgent vs important goals

Make two separate lists of goals. One list should be headed 'urgent goals.' The other should be headed 'important goals.'

Urgent goals	Important goals

Discussion

Urgent items are required to get by. They often involve details such as phone calls, filling out forms, shopping, getting the car fixed, etc. But your 'important goals' list should include 'having a great life, each and every day,' as well as working some kind of big, important, long-term project.

Some important, meaningful projects often include travel, writing, building, creating, loving, caring, etc, etc, but be certain that everything on your 'important goals' list is stated in a way that it can be achieved by effective thinking and doing, rather than by depending on outside events or on the behaviour of others. Remember, you are in charge of your own thinking, but you are most certainly not in charge of outside events or the behaviour of others. Establish goals that are definitely achievable, and not just a matter of good luck, fate, or the good grace of someone outside of your control.

The most important goal in your life, 'a high quality inner existence,' can, of course, be achieved entirely by your own thinking.

Do something a little bit important (make it 'urgent') every day

While many of the things that seem urgent are not really as urgent as they sometimes seem, the doing of something that is on your 'important goals' list is always 'urgent.' Be sure to make steady progress toward the really important goals that you have cut out for yourself.

In order to overcome any tendency you might have to procrastinate, tell yourself that you won't have to do whatever it is that you need to do for very long. Agree that you will only do it for five minutes. For example, if you loathe to clean the house or office, but you know that you should, say to yourself that you will only have to clean for five minutes, no longer, and then you can stop. Then, as so often is the case, after a few minutes, you are likely to have built up some momentum and can use that momentum to work on the job until completion. Paradoxically, by giving yourself a chance to get out of a difficult task, you often can more easily get yourself started and work to completion.

Then, ten years later, you won't have to end up saying 'I'm sorry I never did anything about that important thing that I always intended to do.'

Exercise 8: From this, my short life, I want...

Finish the following sentence stem any way that comes to mind. Then after you have completed a list of wants, place a 'p' near those that you prefer. Place an 'n' next to those that you absolutely need. (It is recommended that you place an 'n' next to those that you can be absolutely sure that you can have, by using effective thinking. All others should be **preferences**. Successful, truly successful people are able to separate their preferences from their **needs**. I hope that you list the pursuit of a full and satisfying life as one of your absolute needs, and not merely a preference.

From this, my short life, I want:

____

Out of my life, I want:

____

Out of my life, I want:

____

continued over

Out of my life, I want:

____

Out of my life, I want:

____

Out of my life, I want:

____

Discussion

Once you know what it is that you really want, you will be able to shape your activities in the finite amount of time accorded you, in a way that helps you realise your objectives. Preferences, not absolute needs are easiest to achieve. So why not try to phrase your needs as strong preferences, if at all possible.

Exercise 9: Inheritance with strings attached

You have just been given by a secret benefactor, the sum of £20 million. But, there is a catch. You must spend all of this money on yourself over the next year and you are not permitted to give any of it to charity or to family, you cannot invest it or buy property and you can only spend this money on yourself. What would you spend this sum on?

____

____

____

____

____

____

Discussion

Don't be alarmed if you run out of ideas. An enormous supply of money is not usually the answer to having the full and satisfying life that you are encouraged to relentlessly seek.

Relentlessly seek

Once you have studied chapters one and two, you should be clear about what it is that you genuinely want out of this short life of yours. If now you are determined to relentlessly seek to have 'a full and satisfying life, but not at the expense of any other person,' you are ready to use programme one.

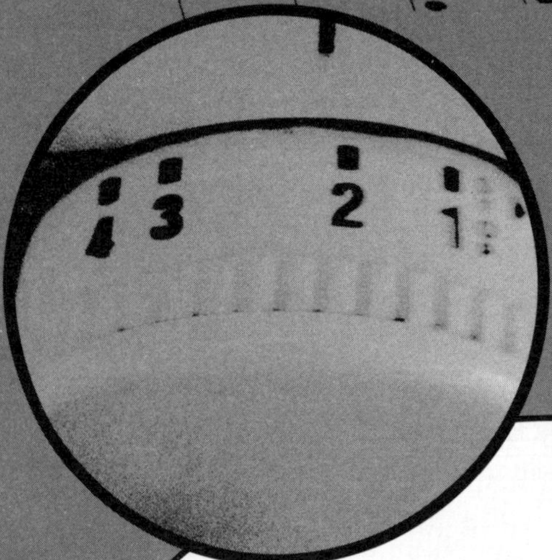

PROGRAMME TWO

'Proactively choose thoughts that provide you with a full and satisfying life, but not at the expense of others.'

Chapters 3 to 11 open the door to complete understanding of how you get your mind to work for you by effective something. Using what you learn in those chapters will provide you with the kind of life I assume you now seek – 'a full and satisfying life, but not at the expense of any other person.'

THREE
Understanding your thought processes

The ticket to the full and satisfying life that I have been urging you to seek is achieved by *taking full charge of your thinking* – the main tenet of effective thinking. If your life is to be a great one, it becomes essential that you take *total self-responsibility* – not for everything going on in this world, but everything going on *from your neck, up*.

The one thing in this world that you, as a human being, can definitely manage is the thoughts that you choose. Interestingly, no other creature, except a human being has the ultimate power to choose any thought he or she wants, at any time and at any place. Lions and tigers do not have free will. Nor do mice. The lower forms of animals are totally products of conditioning and instincts. As human beings, we are products of conditioning and instinct as well, but if a human really wants to, he or she can transcend his or her own conditioning and instinct, with the proper know-how. Let me explain.

Transcending your own social and genetic programme, if need be

There is no way, short of brain surgery, by which anyone can get physically inside your head and *make* you choose a particular thought. They can try, of course, and many people certainly do. But the final choice of what it is that you think is totally yours. Another person can try in the most articulate manner possible to convince you to think a particular thought, but even the most articulate person in the world cannot force you to choose what he/she suggests or urges. Others, or outside circumstances, may influence what thoughts you choose, but in the final analysis the choice is always left to you. Accordingly, you have a tremendous amount of personal power reserved for you, but at the same time, you have an awesome responsibility for the way you choose to live your life.

Effective thinkers know how to transcend, whenever necessary, their social and even their genetic programme and they do so, from time to time, whenever conditions warrant. One's genetic programme is installed at birth and one's social programme is installed in the first five or six years of life – the so called 'formative years.' It is because of your social programme that certain thoughts leap to the forefront of your mind, but with a combination of the will power that you have and a rapid kind of self-hypnosis that I will share with you later, you will be able to choose any thought you desire, and at any time and in any place.

The same holds true with your genetic programme.

Consider the problem of obesity, which so many persons suffer. There are millions of people who have moved unsuccessfully from one diet to another for most of their adult lives. Some experts, for instance, have suggested that certain people have inherited a genetic programme of more fat cells than others. They often blame these abundant fat cells, more than anything else, for becoming and remaining overweight.

You put the food in your own mouth

If you keep clearly in mind that you cannot get fat (under normal circumstances) without putting fattening foods in your own mouth and chewing and digesting them all by yourself, then you cannot realistically blame fat cells (your genetic programme) or even the delicious looking cake, the dessert table, or anything else for choosing thoughts that caused you to eat the fattening food. After all, as adults no one has forced food into our mouths.

It is our thoughts that victimise us if we over-eat. But fortunately, we can learn how to choose thoughts that work on our behalf instead of against us. Naturally, this takes some practice.

One of my clients lost a great deal of weight by applying effective thinking to her over-eating problem. Her food nemesis was raisin bread. But once she began to imagine *that the raisins in the bread were moving (!!)*, she rapidly stopped eating so much raisin bread and lost more than 25 pounds.

Our lives are composed of a finite number of 'present moments.' During each of these moments you are busy choosing thoughts of one sort or another, consciously and unconsciously. Whenever you find that what you are experiencing is less than satisfying or that your behaviour seems self-defeating, you can wilfully select alternate thoughts, more effective thoughts, that permit you access to more effective ways of behaving. Is it not reassuring to know that when necessary you can learn to take charge of your feelings and behaviour simply by selecting more effective thoughts?

Thoughts create feelings

It is well established in medicine that without a correlative thought you can have no feeling. It is the thought that you choose *after* nerve impulses are sent to your brain that suggests to you what is going on – what you should (or should not) feel. Your thought says, in a very real sense, 'That's a feeling that you have going on there. Say, that feeling is one of pain. Ouch!'

Then you look down and notice that you've stepped on a drawing pin. However, without the thought, there would be no such feeling at all. Anaesthetists learned long ago how to block these nerve messages to the brain so that surgeons can operate on us when we are wide awake, under the influence of a local anaesthetic.

Did you ever find yourself avoiding a car accident by instinctively turning the wheel or applying the breaks without a thought of fear at the moment that you took this instantaneous action? Then, perhaps many minutes after it was over, you got the shakes. Obviously, it was *the thoughts* you chose *after the fact* that created the emotional response – in this case fear – manifested by your shaking. So it is with all of your feelings: no correlative thought, then no feeling. Without thoughts you would be little more than a vegetable. Therefore in order to feel good, it is necessary to concentrate on thought choice rather than feelings per se.

If a good friend of yours dies but you have not heard about it, would you be depressed? Of course not. But if two days after the death of your friend, you receive a fax informing you of his/her death, you get very upset and depressed. Was it the event of the death of your friend that upset you, or was it the thoughts about your friend's death, two days later when you read the fax? Of course, it was your thoughts about the death of your friend, not his/her actual death that upset you, not the event. So it is with every feeling we have. It is the thoughts that produce the feeling, not the event.

Who chooses your thoughts?

You do of course.

During one of my recent seminars, I asked this question and a 35 year old manager said: 'My mother chooses my thoughts.' I said, 'If that's the case, I'm a therapist, I'll treat your mother and you'll get better.' But in truth, it doesn't work that way. In every case, we and we alone, ultimately choose our own thoughts. Viktor Frankl was absolutely right when he wrote in *Man's Search for Meaning*: 'the ultimate freedom of man is to choose his own attitude.'

Thoughts create behaviour

Your thoughts are also the key to the way you behave. You cannot possibly pick yourself up and walk from one spot to another and then sit down without the appropriate correlative thoughts. Did you ever see a chicken with its head cut off? Running around in circles. Total aimlessness. The thought that sets your body in motion may take only an instant, but it is a thought nonetheless.

If you act nicely to someone, it is because you choose certain thoughts that enable you to act that way. You may have thought, 'I like so and so, so I will be very kind.' Or perhaps you chose thoughts that were a bit devious. 'So and so has the power to do me a favour. I'll be very gracious to him.' In any case, it is your thought choices that give rise to most of your behaviour. Since thought choice is so powerful a factor in your life, it is well worth mastering.

Your thoughts are the master key to the doors of feelings and behaviour. It is your feelings of course, which are most 'real' to you, which enable you to feel 'good... indifferent,' or 'bad.' It is within the realm of your feelings that you really live. Your behaviour, on the other hand, as important as it is, is much like the tip of an iceberg, merely the part that goes public.

Do not be discouraged if you find yourself adamantly resisting taking responsibility for your thoughts. After all, it is more than likely that for most of your life you have been taught (and told time and time again, since it is deeply ingrained in popular folklore) that it was the external condition that caused you to think a certain way. You will have to fight the natural temptation to fall back on this convenient myth.

However, when you eventually develop the habit of saying, and more importantly of thinking, with conviction, 'Neither she, he, they, nor it made me feel this way, but rather I have chosen thoughts that made me feel this way,' you will be well along the way towards self-management. You must at first remind yourself at regular intervals (acknowledging but overcoming your natural resistance) that it is you who choose thoughts to create your feelings. Doing so will give you access to exciting new options in the way that you live your life.

A thought for your files (*choose one*)

DEFECTIVE THOUGHT

My boss hurt my feelings.

EFFECTIVE THOUGHT

I chose thoughts about my boss that ended up hurting my feelings.

What I do recommend is that when you find yourself feeling or acting in ways that are proving unsatisfactory, you remind yourself loudly and clearly that it is you who are choosing the thoughts that are making you feel or behave so disadvantageously. Of course it is you who can choose other, more effective thoughts if you really care to do so. As a result, you are left with little room to ever say that you've been 'brainwashed.' And although your dreams and fantasies may seem beyond your control at times, you must acknowledge that they take place inside your head. If any person is to be in charge of these fantasies, it must be you and no one else.

GETTING WHAT YOU DESERVE

Effective thinker: 'I don't know if you've heard about it. I recently got a very big assignment, a terrific new job. A very big job. The biggest I have ever had.'

Colleague: 'Marvellous. Good for you. What's it all about?'

Effective thinker: 'Well, you'll never believe this. This new assignment was just an offer that I couldn't refuse.'

Colleague: 'Tell me about it. I'm very curious.'

Effective thinker: 'I've just been appointed Managing Director!'

Colleague: 'Fantastic. Managing Director in charge of what?'

Effective thinker: '*Managing director in charge of me*. See, I told you it was a very big job. It's undoubtedly the biggest job I've ever had in my entire life. I'm in charge, full charge, of a human being's life. That's some responsibility! It scares me a little. But let me tell you, I can't refuse the job. The pay is marvellous. I get paid exactly what I deserve. You can't ask for anything fairer than that. When I really do right by myself, I get rewarded accordingly. When I foul up, of course there's the proper deduction for that, too. After all, I don't expect something for nothing. I like this arrangement because I know that I'll do a good job. I'm a worker. This is the first job where the rewards are perfectly fair, and that's all I ever wanted. Fair chance.'

Certainly this is an *effective way* of viewing the taking of responsibility for oneself, which brings us to the next chapter – the building of one's *effective thought* files.

FOUR

Building your own effective thought file

As you must know by now, the definition of an effective thought is 'any thought (positive, negative, or otherwise) that leads directly or indirectly to you having a rich and satisfying life, but not at the expense of any other person.'

If a thought that you choose doesn't do that, then it is deemed *defective* instead of *effective*. It is your defective, self-defeating thoughts which account for most of your problems: problems at home, at work, in social situations.

The power of thought choosing

You might want to blame that tediously slow driver in front of you, the one hogging the road, for making you angry, but in reality, he doesn't even know you. He probably doesn't even know you exist. No, the truth of the matter is that it is your thoughts, anger-producing thoughts, that are making you angry. You choose and are totally responsible for your thoughts while you are driving. You are capable of choosing, at any time, in any place, all kinds of emotion-producing thoughts, joy-producing thoughts, nerve-wracking thoughts and all kinds of thoughts.

Your thoughts can excite you

That attractive person across the room is not in any way responsible for the thoughts that you choose to think. It is your own thoughts that can 'turn you on' or ' turn you off.'

No more boring meetings – ever

You have no boring meetings to attend at work. It is only you who will be to blame if you bring boring thoughts to the meeting. Simply prepare yourself in advance with interesting, portable, inconspicuous material that you can choose to think about if external things are of no significant value to you.

Not a matter of right or wrong

An effective thought is a thought that works on your behalf to provide you with a full and satisfying life. Since you are free to choose any thought that you like, choosing an *effective* thought can serve you in much better fashion than simply choosing a so-called 'right' thought. For the effective thinker, there is no such thing as right-thinking people and wrong-thinking people. Instead, he/she tends to look at thoughts in terms of whether they are effective or ineffective, or productive or counter-productive.

RIGHT ARTHUR AND WRONG WILLIAM

Arthur, a project manager, was victimising himself by his 'right' thinking. Arthur came to me seeking advice on how to how to deal with his boss, William. 'William is never on time with his end of a deal. He is slower than treacle and it's driving me crazy. Sure we meet the deadline, but his style (procrastination) is driving me crazy and I'm at the point where I'm going to have to quit this job – even though there are many things I really like about it. And after all, I have been here for ten years.'

'Since you have tried to change William and have not succeeded up until now, then why don't you try changing your own attitude about William's procrastinating ways? After all, at least you can manage your own opinion.' I said.

In this case, neither Arthur nor his boss was 'right.' There are various ways to get the job done, and since the deadline was being met, neither William nor Arthur was wrong. In fact they both were equally effective, but since Arthur was getting himself upset, it was his job to choose effective thoughts about William's procrastinating style.

RIGHT SPENCER AND WRONG DORSEY

> Two business partners, Spencer and Dorsey were in a manufacturing business together for over 15 years. They had serious disagreements and came to my consultation firm for some help. Shortly after coming for consultation, Spencer wrote me a letter. He asked me to put in writing who was 'right.' 'Dorsey keeps saying that you told him that I was wrong. I told him that I distinctly heard you say our problems were because of his attitude toward the workers on the factory floor.' I reminded Spencer that it was hardly an issue of right or wrong and that rather, both parties played a part. It was the system that had defects in need of repair, not necessarily one party being right or wrong.

It is important to remind yourself periodically that you have the responsibility to choose effective thoughts that work on your behalf rather than so-called right thoughts.

No thought is unthinkable

The full appreciation of the fact that nothing you ever choose to think at any time is 'unthinkable,' can free you to choose some highly imaginative and original thoughts. And why not? It's your mind and you can think anything that you want to think. Why not choose the most effective thoughts possible?

Be precise in the conversation you have with yourself

One of the most important conversations you can ever have is the conversation that you have with yourself. In these conversations with yourself, the meaning of a word or two can make a tremendous difference in the way you think and consequently feel and act.

The vocabulary that you use to do your thinking can sometimes be much too imprecise. This imprecision can lead to serious misunderstandings.

Take the well-worn maxim, 'think positively.' Positive thinking, if used too loosely, can lead to some treacherous, self-defeating errors in behaviour. Actually there are two types of positive thinking. The distinctions are extremely important. There is *realistic* positive thinking and unrealistic (Pollyanna-like) positive thinking, and misunderstanding this difference causes your errors in behaviour.

In the insurance business it is common practice to analyse how many calls are, on average, necessary to produce one sale. Company records may show that a salesman can expect to make approximately one sale for every ten prospects seen. Now, supposing two different salesmen go out and approach their prospects, 'thinking positively.' Is it reasonable to assume that both men interpret 'think positively' in the very same way? Of course not. Are you referring to realistic positive thinking or unrealistic (Pollyanna-like) positive thinking?

DON'T BE POLLYANNA POSITIVE

> The realistic positive thinking salesman will make his ten calls and one sale, as will the unrealistic positive-thinking salesman. But the realistic positive-thinking salesman will have a much better time of it. He will approach his day's work with this attitude: 'I'll make my ten calls, give ten good sales' presentations, possibly be rejected nine times and probably make one sale.' However, the Pollyanna salesman will have a much more brutal day. He will think like this: 'I'm going to make a sale every time I give a talk. Think positive, think positive.' He is statistically bound to be rejected nine times

out of ten, the same as his co-workers. But at each rejection he will be jolted. Consequently, he will be very exhausted. Positive thinking is far too vague a term to be used indiscriminately.

Dealing with loss

If you suffer a loss of any kind, on or off the job, it's absolutely imperative that you go through a 'grieving process.' Elizabeth Kubler-Ross, an expert on bereavement who has written extensively on the topic of 'death and dying' has enumerated five rather well-known steps inherent in the mourning process:

1. **Denial** 'I can't believe my loved one has died.'
2. **Bargaining** 'Please come back to me.'
3. **Anger** 'I think all this is very wrong and I'm furious.'
4. **Depression** 'I feel really low and deprived.'
5. **Healthy Acceptance** 'Well, enough suffering, it is time to get on with my life.'

Working through a loss of any kind

Before one arrives at a level of healthy acceptance (a most desirable state) over any loss, be it a loss of a loved one, loss of a job, a marriage, a relationship (or even the loss of a file or report!), it is quite necessary to go through denial, bargaining, anger and depression. Certainly, getting angry or depressed is not positive, but in the working through of a loss, getting angry and depressed can prove very effective. Effective thinking managers, therefore, quite deliberately choose thoughts to make themselves depressed or angry when they experience loss in their own life so that they can expedite their eventual acceptance of that loss.

I have found it extremely effective to have my clients use these very same grieving steps to 'work-through' all kinds of losses and setbacks in both business and in personal life.

Some losses in business

- Losing a contract
- Missing out on a sale
- Getting fired
- Not being appreciated
- Not being sufficiently rewarded

The above are losses that hurt, especially if they were not of your fault. It is necessary to grieve in order to get over them. Of course, losses in one's personal life (sickness, financial woes, death, divorce, accidents etc.) all require the same five steps of mourning as well. The goal of working-through is to reach a level of psychological acceptance of the loss and then get on with one's life.

Effective thinking requires that you change your perception of a given situation in such a way that will have maximum payoff for you. That doesn't mean that you'll just accept anything that happens to you. What it does mean is that you'll rapidly accept those things that you can do nothing about and preserve your energy to do the things that you can do something about (and there are many). There is a famous saying that can prove effective at such times:

> ***Give me the courage to change those things that I can change.***
>
> ***Give me the strength to accept those things over which I have no control.***
>
> ***And give me the wisdom to know the difference.***

A starter file of effective thoughts

Below is a starter file of some thoughts that I have found very effective at times. Please note that a thought that may prove effective at one point in time, may not prove effective in another. Also, the thoughts that might be effective for one person, might not be effective for another. You may wish to add to this file some thoughts of your own that you have discovered to be personally effective. Then when it becomes time for you to choose an effective thought to help you with a particular situation, you can refer to this thought file as a starting point. If you don't find exactly what you need here, create for yourself the thought that is needed. When you are through with a particular effective thought for the moment, don't discard it, file it here for future reference, as a periodic reminder of what works for you.

Aloneness

You can sometimes get very close to other persons, but in actuality there will always be a part of you that is totally alone.

There is a big difference between feeling lonely and being alone. Coming to terms with one's fundamental existential loneliness is important. We are fundamentally alone. The way to come to terms with loneliness is to grieve for it – denial, bargaining, anger, depression and then healthy acceptance of it. By embracing loneliness and not running away from it, you will move from feeling lonely and alienated to feeling alone and in touch.

Approval

You cannot ever be fully responsible for what another person thinks about you.

Other persons are responsible for their own thoughts, just as you are for yours. Although you can enjoy having others approve of you, you can never rely on them to do so. If you act primarily for the sake of approval of others, you might very well end up pleasing no one, but if you act in a way that you, yourself, approve of, then at least one person will be pleased! That one person is you, of course.

Body

Your body, as well as your mind, has intelligence. It speaks to you – if you listen to it.

You body (feelings) will tell you whether you are enjoying yourself or not. It will tell you when you are healthy or sick. Your body is the barometer of the sum total of your thoughts, feelings and behaviour. You, not any doctor or any other person, is the best judge of what your body is telling you. Listen to it. And if you want to improve your body, improve your mind. Learning from the 'neck down' begins from the 'neck up'.

Caring about yourself

Most people don't care about you nearly as much as you can care about yourself.

You'd worry a whole lot less about what people are thinking of you if you only knew how rarely they did. This kind of thinking can help you to ease up on any inflated sense of self-importance you might have. It can keep you humble when appropriate. It can help you to ease any pressure you might feel to attempt to sustain a good impression in the eyes of others at all times. It is quite likely that 'others' think about you a whole lot less than you think they do. 'Others,' you must realise, are usually just as busy as you are, focusing essentially on themselves and their own pressing issues.

Caring about rejection

You cannot possibly be rejected by anyone who doesn't listen and care for you on your own terms.

If a person doesn't really listen to you on your own terms, and doesn't really care for you, they don't really know you. And if they don't really know you, they (not you) have a problem. If they don't really know you – then it is not you that they are rejecting. They are merely rejecting their limited perception of you – your image, in their eyes – and that is their own projection. Consequently, the real you can never be rejected, unless the person doing the so-called rejecting knows the real you. The only way to get to know the real you is to really listen and care for you without judging you. If someone were to really listen and care for you *on your own terms without judging you,* then they would be bound to appreciate and perhaps even love you.

Cemeteries

The cemeteries are filled with indispensable people.

We egotistically believe that the world just can't get along without us, but it will get along fine, long after you are gone. There will always be someone who will gladly take your place, and in fact, they may do an even better job than you did. You are not indispensable. No one is. So take time out to enjoy this relatively short life of yours and if you are fortunate enough to have some money, please don't save all of it for a rainy day. Remember, there are no pockets in a shroud.

Centring

You cannot do everything, so edit your life.

It is wise to edit your existence, day by day. You have a '**centre**', if you allow yourself to experience it. Pause and notice your **physical** 'centre' periodically. Just below the region of your heart. Also pause periodically and notice your **psychological and spiritual** 'centre', as well. Around the 'centre', you can integrate everything whether it be inner calm, purpose and adventure. You can discover what you are really about: your own tastes, your own values. You can have your 'centre' come into harmony with your surroundings. Pause and 'centre' frequently each day. Concentrate on quality.

Changing the world

If you really want to change the world for the good, then change yourself.

Idealists want to make this world a better place. If you want to change the world, you can do so. *Change yourself* and you will have changed the world a little bit. After all, you are part of this world, and if you can make yourself a little better as a person, you will have improved the quality of life in this world as well. By taking total self-responsibility, you will have made this crazy world of ours just a little bit better.

Culture

Aim to have more culture and less civilisation in your life.

If you find certain aspects of what we call 'civilisation' getting on your nerves, move into appreciating the cultural aspects of life. Sometimes so called 'civilisation' is not very civil: pollution, rushing about, abuse of nature, heightened materialism, too much technology etc, etc. If this gets on your nerves, consider deepening your understanding and appreciation of culture: the arts, music and an increased sense and understanding of history.

Cynicism

Be a healthy sceptic and not a self-sabotaging cynic.

This thought will keep you from over-reacting when you get discouraged. It will keep you from dropping an entire project, instead of just the part that is not good. Remember 'pause' and 'wait and see.' If you were to be a cynic, you might 'throw out the baby with the bath water.' As a healthy sceptic, you will keep the baby, but discard the dirty water.

Death

You are definitely going to die in a relatively short time.

Even if you live a century, since it is estimated that the world as we know it will last for about nineteen billion years, your lifetime is only 'a drop in the ocean.' You will be in proverbial eternity for a long, long time. No exception will be made in your case, no matter how well connected you are or become. Use your acceptance of this harsh reality as the impetus to make the most of each remaining day that you have.

Drama of life

Think of yourself as participating in a real life drama, not just the 'theatre' of life.

The 'drama' of life is much different from the 'theatre' of life. Theatre, as entertaining as it may be, is artificial. In the theatre, you sit in the audience and watch, but life is real. If you want to live a full life, participate actively in the drama of everyday life rather than stand on the sidelines, watching others live, with you living only vicariously as a theatrical observer. Take chances. Be active. **Play** sports, don't just watch as a fan.

Experience

No one other than you can experience your life.

You can attempt to live vicariously through others by watching TV, dreaming, reading novels, seeing movies, or the like. However, it is quite possible for you to do many things firsthand in your own lifetime if you so choose and if you take appropriate risks. Whose life is it anyway? Remember, your feelings are real. Selectively experience as much as makes sense, in this relatively short life of yours.

Failure

Believe that you never have real 'failures,' just 'learning opportunities.'

When you fail, you discover limits. If you never experience failure, then you do not know what your limits are. If you have never 'failed,' you are probably operating at far less than your capacity. You can turn a so-called 'failure' into a learning opportunity if you learn from your mistakes. Of course, too many 'learning opportunities' can be dispiriting. If you remind yourself that what failed is not you, but simply one of your projects, you will find so-called failing much more acceptable.

Fairness

Remember, the world as it is presently constructed, is just not a very fair place.

Life can sometimes be unfair. Sometimes bad people do well. Other times, bad things happen to good people. You can fight for justice, but some things cannot be remedied. When unfairness strikes, sometimes the only thing left for you to do is to grieve and then get on with your life. Denial, bargaining, anger, depression and then a healthy acceptance.

Fear

All anger stems from fear. Eliminate the fear and you'll eliminate the anger.

All of your wayward emotions stem from fear. Remind yourself to figure out what it is that you are afraid of when you get too angry. If you find that the fear was unnecessary (as is so often the case, especially when you become a master of the effective thinking process), you will feel your anger immediately evaporate. If you get angry, ask yourself what it is that you are afraid of. When you encounter an angry person, don't think – 'what a tough person!' – think 'What is he or she afraid of?'

Feelings

You own a marvellous sensory apparatus. Feelings are strictly a product of the thoughts that you choose. And you can choose any thought you want, at any time and at any place.

Learn to feel. Feelings take place in the here and now. Still, it is your thoughts that produce all of your feelings. Without a thought, you have no feeling. You can choose thoughts that deepen and enrich your emotional life. You can learn how to see more effectively, hear more clearly, smell more keenly, move more gracefully, and feel more sensitively. You can enrich your moment-by-moment existence at literally no cost to you or anyone else, simply by taking time out and choosing to pay attention to what it is that you are feeling.

The future

Remind yourself periodically, 'the best is yet to come.'

It is true that the future is not what it used to be. 'The best is yet to come' is a very effective thought to have about your future. Whether that is really true can never be assured, but it is an effective way to think about your prospects.

When life is going well, there is little pressure to dream about a better future. Certainly it is wise to make the most out of each present moment that you have, but if making a present moment rich and satisfying is difficult (because things are going badly) then why not make that present moment rich and exciting by having hope. Hope for the future can make any present moment better. The one thing that is often greater than pleasure itself is the anticipation of pleasure. So why not say to yourself, 'the best is yet to come.'

Gamesmanship

In business, it is better for you to be good at gamesmanship instead of at jungle warfare.

Sometimes it pays to lose a battle in order to win the war. Life is serious, but business is a game. Play the game of business to win. Sometimes the straight line is not the shortest distance between two points. Have fun and adventure playing in the game of business. Do not be a simple and crude jungle-fighter. Be smarter than that.

Grieving in advance

You can always grieve in advance for your own demise and then, by minimising your fear of death, really begin to live.

If you haven't accepted the harsh fact that you are going to die someday, then it is time to do so – right away. Go though the grieving process: denial, bargaining, anger, depression, and finally arrive at a healthy level of acceptance. By grieving in advance for your own death or any other loss, you will be able to free yourself of the fear of that loss and you will then be able to get on with your life instead of spending too many of your finite waking moments filled with worry.

Guilt

Guilt before the fact has value. Guilt after the fact has no value unless you can make reparations.

What is done is definitely done. There is no going back. It makes sense to learn from your errors so as not to repeat them, but nothing worthwhile is accomplished by self blame over that which cannot be rectified. You cannot possibly go back in time.

It is useful to feel guilty before, but not after, you do something wrong. This 'guilt-in-advance' can stop you from doing something that is wrong, but guilt after you have already done something wrong makes little sense, unless you can still make reparations. If you can make reparations, be sure to make them. However, actually 'going back' is impossible, since life is not a movie. Forgive yourself for past mistakes or indiscretions, but also avoid repeating any erring ways that you might have had in the past.

Holism

You are all of one piece.

Your mind and body are one. Your thoughts, feelings, and behaviour are all of one piece. Remember, your thoughts are 'the key to your existence,' your feelings are 'where you really live,' and it is your behaviour which is in essence 'that small tip of the iceberg that goes public.' By choosing effective thoughts, instead of defective thoughts, you will have effective feelings and behaviour. Then, putting thoughts, feelings and behaviour together, you will be whole.

Humour

Life is much too serious to not have a sense of humour about it.

The world is a little bit crazy, so don't take it so seriously. Go a little bit crazy before you are driven crazy. Laugh at life and then enjoy it. You will never fully understand it. No one does. If someone claims to do so, who are they kidding? You know very well, that seeing the stupidity in much of what we all seem to take so seriously can actually help you to enjoy even the most difficult aspects of many events.

Hurting

Allowing yourself occasionally to become 'hurt and vulnerable' is the price of your periodic admission into the family of humankind.

With all of the power that will accrue to you because of your consistent use of effective thinking it will sometimes be necessary to allow yourself to become vulnerable and hurt. It is not effective to distance yourself from all of the pain that exists. Allowing yourself to become vulnerable and feel pain will put you in touch with the family of humankind.

Some of your most productive and original thinking can take place while feeling low, hurt, depressed and vulnerable. Being too cold or too cheerful (where it gets on other people's nerves) is a product of *defective* thought-choosing, not *effective* thought-choosing.

Hypocritical behaviour

On specific occasions, give yourself special permission to be a hypocrite.

There is no law against giving yourself permission to be a hypocrite. Allowing yourself to be a hypocrite from time to time allows you, for example, to accept the compliments other people may give you, but when necessary, to reject any blame that they might throw your way. Admittedly this is inconsistent, but it works and if doing it is not at the expense of another person, do it. For example, if you are credited with being a brilliant and fascinating speaker, don't say to yourself, 'No, it is just that they were an excellent audience and I'm not responsible for their positive response. They choose their own thoughts, just as I do.' No, take the credit if something positive is offered. Enjoy being an effective hypocrite.

Identity

You have a hidden inner identity that goes beyond your job title or even your family role.

Access your hidden identity as needed. How to do this is explained in the pages ahead. Your hidden identity has the elements of inner calm, purpose and adventure structured into it. As we've discussed, these three ingredients are all that are needed in order to have great life satisfaction. Remind yourself of your hidden identity periodically. This hidden identity of yours will insulate you from fear of losing your job or having your family role brought into question. You will have little to fear if you lose a job title, or become hurt by changes in the organisation that you serve. It will keep you from becoming unduly upset during family strife.

Jealousy

All jealousy is based on fear.

A person becomes jealous if he or she fears that they will not get their fair share of whatever it is that he or she is jealous about. If you remind yourself that you are 'special and unique' and *incomparable*, you will see your jealousy rapidly disappear. Stop making onerous comparisons. In order to reduce jealousy, it is essential to first acknowledge that you have it. Some jealousy can be a good thing if it provides you with a worthwhile competitive spirit.

Life purpose

The main purpose of life is to make it as full and as satisfying as possible, but not at the expense of any other person.

Your mission is to have a full and satisfying life, but not at the expense of any other person. It is a valid purpose of life to have a great life, especially if it is not at the expense of others and by you having such a life, you stand as a marvellous example to others, especially to your family and those close to you. You also stand as an example for those that work with and alongside you.

Life satisfaction

You will be better off and have a much higher quality of existence if you pursue 'satisfaction,' rather than 'happiness.'

Remind yourself that 'the pursuit of happiness' is not a worthy and sufficient goal when compared to striving for a 'full and satisfying life.' 'Happiness' does not serve very well as a life objective. Happiness will serve you better as a pleasant by-product that you can sometimes receive as a result of your pursuit of life 'satisfaction.' Happiness is much easier to achieve when you do not aggressively pursue it. It will not be very satisfying for you to be artificially happy.

Martyrdom

Stubbornly refuse ever to feel that you are a victim or martyr.

Be sure to trick yourself back into the driver's seat – even when you really have been temporarily 'victimised.' Effective thinkers can be a victim just like anyone else, but they will not be 'victimised', ie they will not feel that they are a victim for very long. They make it their business to figure out a way of handling any circumstance (good or bad) that life serves-up.

More

You are a fountain of ideas and opportunities.

When you believe that 'there really is more where that came from,' you not only become more generous, you also become more productive. Effective thinkers know that when it comes to ideas, they are a fountain with an unlimited supply of effective thoughts at their disposal, so they can give more, and consequently, receive more. As a result, they are generous, prolific and prosperous. By thinking of themselves as an endless fountain, they create a very effective self-fulfilling prophecy.

Now

This present moment is all that you can ever be certain about.

'Nows' are all you have ever had, or ever will have. Your past is 'nows' used up. Your future is 'nows yet to come.' This present 'now' is available just for a moment. It is yours to experience as you wish. It will soon be gone. You have only a limited number of present moments allocated to you. The past is gone forever. Your selective-recall processes will distort your memory to protect your ego. The future is not assured in any way. However, if you take care of each 'now' as it comes along, the prognosis for your future is excellent. The future is nothing more than 'nows' sent on ahead and if you have been taking care of your 'nows' as you go along, you will have had an excellent track record. How do you make your 'nows' so good. Simply pause and choose effective thoughts for each 'now' you have.

Ownership

You don't really own anything, until you can comfortably give it away.

This thought will permit you to become more generous if that is what you want to be. You will find that it is true that if you spend too much of your limited time trying to retain a possession, material or otherwise, you will expend much too much energy keeping an eye on it, watching it, caring for it, and making sure that no one takes it away. So, in a very real sense, a possession of that type begins to own you, instead of your owning it. You will find it infinitely easier to 'travel light.' When you give something that you own away, you will have the memory of it forever, and then you will be free to do just as well or even better in another activity. You will find this thought especially useful for giving gifts, sharing ideas, staying 'loose,' being spontaneous, and going through life without much burden.

The past

Take the flames from the past and forget the ashes.

This thought reminds you of the fact that 'the past is already history' and subject to enormous amounts of selective retention. Aim to take the flames, the useful parts of the past and discard the rest, as one might do with ashes. Remember to move forward into the present and future, and yet at the same time, honour the past by taking vital lessons from history.

Purpose

It is much more productive to spend time searching for purpose and meaning than searching for happiness.

Purpose involves loving others or something, even more than yourself. Purpose is also found in making achievements. If you have a 'why' for your existence, then the 'how' becomes secondary. For example, if your purpose is to create a new way of doing something on the job, that purpose will serve to give you the drive to find a way to achieve that objective.

Preferences

Prefer whatever you wish, but need only a very few things.

You must realise that the most difficult time in the world to ever get something is when you really need it. It is useful to convince yourself that you need very little. Couch your deepest desires, not as something that you need, but rather as something that you prefer. You 'need' a certain amount of food, shelter and clothing just to stay physically alive and to keep from freezing. It is effective to 'prefer' more than you need, but it is not effective to be needy. You can 'prefer' a vast wardrobe, and you can 'prefer' a large home, but you don't 'need' more than the minimum.

Prioritising

Regularly edit your life. You can't include everything.

This thought reminds you to establish pecking orders when necessary. It is, of course, impossible for you to do everything equally well, even if you wanted to. It can remind you to focus on quality rather than quantity. It can help you to organise your schedule, limit your commitments and concentrate on genuine, rather than superficial, relationships and activities. It can remind you that your energy is not unlimited. You can't even help others if you drain yourself and, in a sense, bring others an uncharged battery to their assistance. Separate the important from the urgent and do something important almost every day. Edit your life, the same way that you might edit a book or paper that you have written.

Rapid grieving

Use rapid grieving whenever it makes sense to do so.

Grieve more rapidly than most other persons. Do not skip over this essential process whenever you have a setback or loss, just do your grieving quickly. Quickly move beyond 'denial.' Then quickly bargain and try to restore the situation to what it was before the apparent setback. Then, if your 'bargaining' proves to no avail, deliberately get angry and then force yourself to get depressed. The sooner that you do all this, the sooner you will get on with life.

Rationalisation

Have healthy rationalisations, but not unhealthy ones.

You may have believed, if you ever studied psychology, that 'rationalisation' has a negative connotation, that rationalisation is a defence mechanism, but you should also know that there are both healthy as well as unhealthy defence mechanisms. You need healthy defence mechanisms to cope with aspects of this world that are very difficult. In fact the whole effective thinking process is essentially one big healthy defence system for living in and dealing with a difficult (sometimes, quite insane) world.

Realistic expectations

You will be better off if you are 'realistic' and not merely 'reasonable.'

By just being 'reasonable' in this rather irrational world of ours one can experience great frustration. It is much wiser to be 'realistic.' Being realistic requires that you make accurate predictions about what is likely to happen. Being realistic, especially when dealing with people, requires that you make some allowance for human foible, mistakes and errors. Have 'realistic expectations' about your work and about your family life and you will not be disappointed.

Rejection

You cannot possibly be rejected by those who do not really care about you or know you.

If a person does not really care about you, he can't really listen effectively to you. If he/she cannot really listen to you, then it follows that he/she can't really get to know you, at least for what you really are. If he/she does not know you for what you really are, then it is not you that he/she is actually rejecting but rather his/her illusion of you. Therefore, it is difficult to take much so-called rejection seriously.

Relationships

All of your relationships with other persons are conditional. Value given, for value received.

You cannot possibly be all things to all people and you will kill yourself if you try to be. All relationships are conditional. Even your closest friend or your spouse will truly accept you on a conditional basis only. If, for example, you decide to 'cheat' on your spouse, the character of the relationship is bound to change. There is a hierarchy in one's relationships; you value some more than others.

You can clarify your own set of relationships with a pecking order. An example of an interpersonal pecking order is as follows:

1 some larger force
2 self
3 wife and children
4 good friends and colleagues
5 other friends and acquaintances.

You can develop, for example at work, your own pecking order.

Example:

1 your customers
2 the 'big' boss
3 your immediate boss
4 your direct reports
5 your colleagues, etc.

Reputation

Remember, you are not your reputation.

You are not entirely in charge of what others think of you. You might be able, to some extent, to influence what others think of you, but you are definitely not in charge, in the final analysis, of what they end up choosing to think of you. Your image in the eyes of others is your reputation and you are most certainly a lot more than your mere image. Your image lies strictly in the eye of the beholder. You are really your hidden identity.

Risking

You can make life exciting and adventurous by intelligent risk taking.

There is truly danger in the comfort zone. Taking intelligent chances makes life exciting and interesting, but take your risks in harmony with your sense of inner calm and your sense of purpose. Choose thoughts that make you spontaneous and sensual and you will have lots of fun, but not at the expense of others.

Roles

In everyday life you are often required to play various roles.

There is a significant distinction between playing a role and doing a job. Playing the role of manager, for example, can be quite different from the actual act of managing. Playing roles is often necessary, but role-playing by definition is never really a very serious business. Doing a job is not the same as playing a role. One can often do both well, but it is important to be aware of the considerable differences between the two. Never confuse the roles you play with who you really are.

Responsibility for thought-choice

You are totally responsible for the thoughts that you choose, the feelings that these thoughts produce and the subsequent behaviours resulting from those thoughts.

You are responsible for yourself and your actions whether you are able to acknowledge it or not. No one else is ever responsible for what you choose to think (and subsequently feel). You are in charge of your own destiny, whether you want to be or not. Without a thought, you can have absolutely no feelings or meaningful behaviour. Without a brain you are brain dead, a vegetable. Who, in the final analysis chooses your own thoughts? You do, of course. You are responsible for the world, from the neck-up.

The main reason why so many people find this reality difficult to accept is because it takes away the most insidious defence mechanism, ever: ie the desire to blame others for how we think, feel and behave.

Seeking horizons

Aim for a 'horizon' instead of a 'boundary.'

The 'horizon' continuously changes as you move toward it and as you move forward, you should remind yourself that the best is yet to come. You can never really ever expect to reach the horizon, and thus you can keep going until your dying day. The view of the horizon is always from a distance. You will find a 'boundary' limiting, but a 'horizon' a free and open circle.

Suffering

Suffering is optional.

Suffering is strictly a result of thought-choice – and not the external event. Use this concept to remind yourself to suffer sometimes – but not to suffer too much – even when things become painful. You will find the reminder that suffering is optional to be helpful in minimising your pain in the dentist's chair, and also in maximising the general quality of your life, day to day.

Taking charge

You are just in charge of this world, from the neck-up, only.

This thought, the basic premise of effective thinking, will remind you to take self-responsibility in terms of what is going on in your own mind. It will also keep you from pompously trying to manage the minds of others. Taking care of your own mind is a big enough job, in and of itself.

Treatment by others

In the long run people will tend to treat you the way that you teach them to treat you.

You don't have to accept other people's behaviour, especially when it comes to the way that they treat you. A person or an organisation may be allowed to mistakenly mistreat you once, but after that, it is your duty to teach them how to treat you. And you can teach them how to treat you decently and with respect by politely calling them aside and explaining your decency policy in a nice way. If they 'don't get it,' take stronger steps in your education of them on the way to treat you. This applies equally to bosses, colleagues, friends, family, children, clerks and all others that have a connection with your life.

Uniqueness

You are special and unique.

When you were born, the mould was broken and thrown away. There never was a person exactly like you in the history of the world, and there never will one exactly like you, ever again. The 'rhythm' inside you is all your own. You can stop to hear it whenever you want to do so. You can dance to, or march to it as you wish. No one else can hear it. You are not crazy just because others don't hear this music. They have their own, if they will listen for it.This thought will help you to hold on to high self-esteem, even when things get difficult. It will also help you to overcome jealousy. 'I may not have that, but at least I'm me – special and unique.' It will help you to appreciate the fact that you are quite significant and rather unusual and that can keep you from making comparisons with someone else, who, in one way or another might be doing just a little bit better than you are. Just say to yourself: 'Well, we are just in a different league and playing a slightly different kind of game.'

Values

A value is better caught than taught.

Values are deeply felt and if you want to share them, you do better by example than by lecture. Set an example for others that you want to influence: colleagues, bosses, subordinates, children, spouses, clients and friends. Instead of trying to lecture those that you want to influence into your value-laden point of view, use this thought to encourage yourself to set an inspiring example. If you want your child to enjoy reading, you should enjoy reading. If you want your direct subordinates to be enthusiastic about the job, you should be enthusiastic about the job. If you want your colleagues to manage themselves better, why don't you make it your business to manage yourself better – first.

Work vs play

Work hard, but play even harder.

This concept stops you from overusing any 'workaholic' tendencies that you may have. There's nothing at all wrong with working hard, of course, but in order to keep your life priorities clear, remind yourself, periodically that there is certainly more to life than just work.

Many persons do it the other way around and play hard, but work even harder. Whenever you are taking work too seriously, take notice, pause, identify and choose to work hard, but play even harder. It will remind you that your main purpose is to live a life that is uncommonly successful. Some work and achieve plenty of life satisfaction. Interestingly, whenever you don't take your work too seriously, you will usually do it a little better. When you try too hard, you will tend to cramp your own style.

Worry

Replace excessive worry with 'due concern.'

Worry is usually looked upon as a negative and too much of it certainly is. However, a little 'creative worry' or 'due concern' can help you to be a little more sensitive and caring. Due concern will help you to prepare in advance, when it makes sense to do so. It can keep you on your toes. As an effective thinker, you can be very much in charge of your emotions. You can worry 'a little,' when it helps. You can stop worrying when it is useless, simply by replacing worry with due concern.

Worse

It could always be worse than it is.

This is an excellent effective thought, when nothing else is left. If you have a disease, it could always be worse. After all, 'from the day that you are born, till your trip in the hearse, things are never so bad that they couldn't get worse.'

This thought is likely to be one of best all-purpose effective thoughts around to carry you through a tough time, and it is true, things could always be a bit worse. This is a good illustration of a non-positive thought than can be very effective at times. Use as needed. It may serve to lighten the load.

Note: just a beginning

This starter file is just that, a beginning. An effective thought, permit me to remind you, is any thought that works for you in a given instance, positive or negative, brilliant and not so brilliant. Any thought that leads toward the desired result (a better life) is effective.

FIVE
Uncomplicated but effective thoughts

Here are some other thoughts that can prove effective. Notice that some are very obvious, uncomplicated and positive. A thought does not have to be particularly clever, complex or brilliant to produce a full and satisfying life.

Some uncomplicated thoughts that can be 'effective'

On the boss

I enjoy working for my boss (*to enjoy going to work, and working for your particular boss*).

On calming down

I'm on a beautiful beach by the sea (*to relax and enjoy a bit of time*).

On commuting to work

I enjoy commuting to my job. I do some great thinking on the trip (*to help tolerate the long trip to and from work each day*).

On compassion

I'm hurting for the many people that are going to go to bed hungry tonight (*to feel sensitive and caring about the world*).

On concentrating

I'm interested (*to pay more attention and be more attentive*).

On confidence

I feel great. I'm quite wonderful (*to feel self-confident and act outgoing, if appropriate, for the occasion*).

On dieting

I dislike desserts (*to remain on your diet*).

On exhilaration

I'm scoring the winning goal for the team (*to feel exhilarated, excited, or enjoy a bit of time*).

On expansiveness

I see one of the most beautiful scenes that I have ever seen in my entire life (*to feel more expansive, to feel in touch with beauty and larger forces, to feel calmer*).

On fun

I'm enjoying my favourite comedian (*to laugh and feel better*).

On getting even

'Take this! Take that!' (imaginary punching) (*for getting rid of, or at least lessening negative feelings about a particular individual*).

On importance

I'm thinking of the wonderful applause I got after my talk (*to feel important, or proud, or to enjoy a bit of time*).

On modesty

I'm not particularly interesting (*to feel humble and to keep quiet, if appropriate for the occasion*).

On motivation

The enemy is chasing me, I've got to keep moving (*to get your adrenaline flowing*).

On pleasure

I'm thinking of my fantastic son (daughter, friend, lover, etc) (*to feel appreciated, or proud, or to enjoy a bit of time*).

On pomposity

I'm enjoying wearing the crown jewels (*to feel materially rich, and a bit pompous* [why not, once in a while?]).

Pretending

I can always feign illness, anger, joy or indifference (*to avoid being taken advantage of, or to make a sale, or to influence another person in a particular way*).

On prowess in a sport

I'm engaging in my favourite sport and playing like a champion (*to get better at that athletic activity and to feel stronger and more self-confident*).

On public speaking

I love public speaking (*to have confidence when making a presentation*).

On not smoking

I disdain cigarettes (*to quit smoking*).

On vindictiveness

I'm throwing darts at 'so and so' on my imaginary dartboard (*for 'getting even' without really harming the 'so and so' that you have in mind*).

Subtle differences in words

Below are some terms and phrases that generally make the difference as to whether a thought proves effective or not. The wording of a thought can have a major effect on outcome. Use the effective words listed below for optimal results in any 'original' effective thoughts that you identify for yourself. Remember, the secret is to keep control of the difficulty that you face in your own hands, instead of outside of your control. It is absolutely essential that one becomes very precise in the language that one uses in one's thinking. It is a serious error to believe that words don't really make much of a difference. It is not true that the subtle differences in words are mere semantics. Often, the misuse of even one small word can make a major difference.

There is a subtle but major difference between 'preferences' and 'needs,' 'coulds' and 'shoulds,' 'effective thinking' and 'correct thinking.'

> **Precision in the use of words is essential for certain thoughts to be truly effective.**

It is important that you become familiar with these important words and phrases since most of them will appear again in the samplers of effective thoughts that I've provided for you later on in this chapter and in some of the case examples used when we show how effective thinking is put into action.

Following each effective/defective word comparison is the use of those same words in a sentence with an explanation of rationale for using that particular type of wording.

EFFECTIVE WORDS	**DEFECTIVE WORDS**

Preferences — **Needs**

'I prefer it, but I don't really need it.' (*It's easier to get something when you don't really need it. The most difficult time to get a job is when you really need one*).

Learning opportunities — **Failures**

'I don't have failures. Just learning opportunities.' (*A learning opportunity provides you with the impetus to learn from your mistakes, whereas a failure doesn't necessarily imply having the chance to learn for next time around*).

Forgiveness — **Permission**

'I sometimes find it wiser to ask for forgiveness rather than permission.' (*Handy for those occasions when you want to move into action instead of just waiting*).

Scepticism — **Cynicism**

'I'm a sceptic, not a cynic.' (*Cynics tend to throw out the good with the bad. Sceptics distinguish the useful from the useless – and keep the useful*).

EFFECTIVE WORDS	DEFECTIVE WORDS

Realistic positive thoughts — **Pollyanna positive**

'I'm realistic, not Pollyanna' (*Pollyanna means to be naive and simplistic, but 'realistic positive' – suggests facing reality head on*).

Horizons — **Boundaries**

'I reach for the horizon, instead of the boundary.' (*That's because the horizon always changes as we move toward it, keeps one going, but a boundary is limited. Useful in order to view life as a journey rather than a destination*).

Realistic — **Reasonable**

'I'm realistic, not merely reasonable.' (*It sometimes doesn't pay to be reasonable in a world that is often unreasonable. If you have realistic expectations instead of just reasonable expectations you are less likely to be disappointed. Can keep you calm*).

Dramatic — **Theatrical**

'I enjoy the drama of life, not just the theatre of life.' (*'Theatre' suggests being artificial. Drama suggests the real stuff that real life is made of*).

Resonate like a bell — **Explode like a cannon**

'It's often better to resonate, than to explode.' (*To resonate means to move in harmony with, but to explode, means to destroy*).

Influence of others — **Control of others**

'I influence, but do not control others.' (*The truth is that you cannot enter the mind of another, but you can influence the mind of another. This can help the manager be more realistic in his relations with others*).

EFFECTIVE WORDS	DEFECTIVE WORDS

Insufficiently motivated — **Lazy**

'He's not lazy. He's just not motivated enough.' (*This distinction leaves room to do something about the situation instead of just casting blame or labelling. If a person is cast as 'lazy.' that becomes a final label. If he is cast as 'insufficiently motivated', there is the suggestion that something can be done about that*).

I can — **I must**

'It isn't that I must do that. But I can do that, if I want to.' (*'Can' gives you a choice. 'Must' makes it absolute and out of the realm of choice. 'Can' is personally empowering. 'Must' can be imprisoning*).

I choose to be — **I am**

'I choose to be a worrier' is different from 'I am a worrier.' (*Choosing puts the capacity for change in the hands of the chooser*).

I will — **I'll try**

'Not I'll try, but I will.' (*If one just says, 'I'll try,' one has a built-in escape hatch that can keep one from actually doing*).

Make the decision 'right' — **Make the 'right decision'**

'Not make it right, in advance, but after.' (*A distinction that can give you permission to make a decision, even without all of the facts. Excellent concept to help you to avoid excessive procrastination*).

Wise decisions — **Quick decisions**

'Make wise decisions, not just fast ones.' (*Good idea whenever you need to be more contemplative, and avoid rushing*).

Challenged **Handicapped**

'I'm not handicapped by my disease. Just physically challenged.' (*Keeps the control in the hands of the individual in question*).

Why not? **Why?**

'Why not? instead of why?' (*Good, whenever you want to be more proactive, instead of conservative or reactive*).

Could **Should**

'I could, but who says I should?' (*Allows you to question the authority for requiring something.*)

Life satisfaction **Life happiness**

'I seek life satisfaction, which is not necessarily the same as happiness.' (*It can be a 'very satisfying' experience to make a condolence call on someone who has lost a loved one, even though that might not be a 'happy' experience. Happiness is usually better realised as a by-product, of the goal of life satisfaction, rather than an end, in and of itself*).

Effective thought **Correct thought**

'If a particular thought works for me, even if it may be considered stupid, or incorrect – it is effective.' (*This is a basic reminder of an important difference between simply being correct, or being effective. The two are not necessarily the same.*)

Due concern **Worry**

'I have due concern, not worry over that issue. (*'Worry' goes beyond 'due concern' and worry can be non-productive unless used creatively*).

Grieving in advance **Denial**

'I grieve in advance because I'm realistic.' (*Grieving in advance is an excellent method for dealing with the untoward things that are bound to happen to you simply by virtue of being alive and active. Without grieving for a loss, you are destined to be plagued by 'unfinished business'*) .

Suffering is optional **Suffering is inevitable**

'I choose not to suffer.' (*Taking self-responsibility suggests that you can always choose thoughts that make you suffer, or not*).

Anger stems from fear **Anger is 'macho'**

'When I am fearful, I ask myself, what am I afraid of?' (*Getting at the fear that is the basis of one's anger can quickly dispel that anger. Excessive anger can be avoided if one is not excessively fearful and excessive anger is seldom productive*).

Take the flames from the past, and forget the ashes **Do not dwell on the past**

'I take the flames from the past, and then get on with my life.' (*It pays to learn from the past. It even pays to revel in past good times but concentrate on the present*).

SIX

Managing your effective thought files

Once you have a file of effective thoughts ready for choosing, it is necessary to organise your thoughts so that they can be put to work to your advantage. Some of the ways include organising thoughts into 'lines,' or around a situation or specific purpose, or even using an acronym as an effective thought reminder. Let's examine some lines of effective thoughts first.

'Lines' or 'combinations' of effective thoughts

Here's how the contrasting words of preferences v. needs can be used to help you to build a line or battery of effective thoughts, ie stringing together a number of effective thoughts to present a strong case for yourself to deal with a difficulty.

There is a particular line of effective thoughts that can be quite helpful for dealing with one of the harshest realities that we all face, the harsh reality of our own eventual death. It is a fact that your death is unavoidable. By following this line of thinking, you may find that the fact of your eventual demise can be used to give you energy to make more of your remaining days, instead of living in fear. Look upon this life as 'a short vacation from eternity.'

A LINE OF EFFECTIVE THOUGHTS ABOUT LIFE BEING SHORT

Jastrow, the noted space scientist has estimated that this planet of ours will last about 19 billion years.

At the end of that time, the planet earth will get so close to the sun that it will turn into a ball of fire. Also, according to Jastrow, and many other scientists, it is estimated that our planet earth is already about seven billion years vintage. You were in eternity for about seven billion years. Then you were born and you have your three score and ten, or even four or five score years and then you will return to 'eternity.' You'll go back to eternity for an estimated 12 billion more years (according to Jastrow) minus the few years of your life span. Viewed in this manner, your life right now is 'a short vacation from eternity.' Since you are on a relatively 'short vacation,' shouldn't you be sure to enjoy it? Why not make your short vacation uncommonly successful? It makes no sense whatsoever, does it, to spend your 'relatively short vacation from eternity' suffering from great upset.

Some effective thoughts on being treated unfairly

One of the unavoidable facts of life is that each of us now and then, perhaps some more than others, gets mistreated, or treated unfairly. This is just one of the natural hazards of living in society, a basic penalty.

Life, as you must know, can sometimes be extremely unfair.

There are large and small injustices

- You have a major setback.
- You catch a cold when someone else, who deserves it more, doesn't.

- Your car breaks down in the middle of the highway, even though your mechanic just checked it out, said it was perfect, and charged you £150 for his appraisal.
- A colleague at work who has been ducking responsibility gets more praise than you do.
- Your spouse accuses you of extravagance when you've really denied yourself some luxuries.
- Your child tells you 'drop dead' – and after all you've done for him/her!

Lines of effective thoughts about injustice

Justice is such an abstract and relative concept that self managing people have learned how to stop eating their hearts out about the times they don't seem to get a fair deal. In one large global sweep, they have *mourned in advance* for the fact that they are likely to be treated quite unfairly from time to time. They might even cry. Their hearts ache for themselves. It's part of their recognition that, fundamentally, they are unique and sometimes quite alone in this world. They wish they could always be fully appreciated, that they could always get a fair deal, but they come to terms with the fact that life doesn't always work out that way.

This does not, of course, keep them from vigorously pursuing a fair deal, assertively doing all that is necessary to correct an apparent wrong – but they are determined that by all means they will not eat their hearts out if sometimes an obvious wrong cannot be redressed. They just do what they can, but they avoid assiduously 'the *triple* penalty.'

Avoiding the triple penalty

1. The basic penalty, that occasional injustice is sometimes imposed upon us, is not under our own control, but the second and third penalties are totally self-induced.
2. The second penalty encompasses allowing yourself to become internally upset over the injustice that took place.
3. The third penalty involves hurting yourself still further while trying to 'get even.'

The following case illustrates how a person can foolishly take all three penalties instead of just one.

JOHN TAKES THE TRIPLE PENALTY

John uses his hard-earned cash for an air conditioner from Friendly Franchise, Inc. When the air conditioner arrives, it is useless. He writes to the company president. Still no satisfaction. (By now, poor John realises that he has been taken.) This represents the basic penalty, unavoidable sometimes, even by the best of us.

While John takes those steps necessary to be redressed for this obvious wrong, he is filled with anger: he is irritated and annoyed. He loses sleep, he yells at his kids, he bemoans his fate. 'Damn that Friendly Franchise. What crooks!' All of John's anger and fury (turned inward on himself) represents the second penalty, a penalty that was totally unnecessary for him to inflict upon himself. Self managing persons never take the second penalty, because they have learned how to choose the effective thoughts to prevent such useless anger and frustration.

Meanwhile, Friendly Franchise has a special offer on the very TV set that John has been shopping around for, for months. Friendly Franchise is legitimately selling this set for £100 less than all the competition. Furthermore, the set is fully guaranteed by the manufacturer. However, John (in spite) thumbs his nose at this opportunity and pays the extra £100 at another store. He has now taken the third penalty, just about all that he can get. He has spited himself in order to get even. A successful effective thinking manager *never* spites himself in order to get even unless he has weighed the advantages and disadvantages.

In other words, effective thinkers might get hurt every now and then, but by choosing the necessary effective thoughts they always manage to greatly minimise their loss. This option is open to everyone. Imagine a world in which so much of the anguish was eliminated overnight, where no one upset themselves unnecessarily, and where getting even while spiting oneself rarely took place. What a human ecological event that would be. There is little hope, however, that everyone will operate that way. It is an individual choice.

A thought for your files (*choose one*)

DEFECTIVE THOUGHT

How did my car break down in the middle of nowhere? Bad luck. A rotten deal. I feel miserable and angry.

EFFECTIVE THOUGHT

Ouch. Look at this strange place where my car broke down. I sometimes set myself up for stupid circumstances. I'll get angry for a while (rapid grieving) and then I'll quickly figure how I can turn this mess around.

Organise effective thoughts for specific purposes

I have found that by organising certain relevant effective thoughts in a particular way serves various special purposes. In conducting a seminar on total effectiveness, I selected ten powerful thoughts to share. I called them the ten imperatives and I will review them below:

THE TEN EFFECTIVE THINKING IMPERATIVES

1. Be realistic, not merely reasonable
2. Take charge of yourself, at least from the neck-up
3. Use effective, rather than defective, thinking
4. Influence others, but control yourself, especially your thought-choices
5. Pursue satisfaction, not happiness
6. Be careful what you choose to pursue
7. Use your hidden identity (to be explained later)
8. Seek good stress, not toxic distress
9. Avoid self-defeating mindsets
10. Reinvent yourself, whenever necessary

You, of course, will recognise them. They were all taken from the starter file of effective thoughts that we discussed earlier. Still they bear repeating. One can never get enough reminding of effective thoughts. The reason for repeating them here is to demonstrate another interesting way to remind yourself of thoughts that might work on your behalf.

Consider using an acronym as a reminder

For a short talk on self-management that I gave, I organised four very useful thoughts in the form of an acronym. When pausing, consider thinking to yourself: P-R-E-P. PREP stands for a series of four effective thoughts that can prove extremely useful almost any time you find you are not having a very satisfying time.

Pause and 'PREP'

- **P** stands for 'prefer' don't 'need.'
- **R** stands for be 'realistic,' not merely 'reasonable.'
- **E** stands for strive for excellence, not perfection.
- And the final **P** in PREP stands for, have a 'project,' rather than a 'problem.'

Practice giving yourself some effective advice

Practice giving yourself self managing advice, sound, effective thoughts to choose in each of the following situations:

Exercise

Your boss hauls you over the coals for not doing all you can on the job

Some effective thoughts for this:

____

____

____

____

Your spouse tells you that you are not participating sufficiently in the responsibilities of running the household.

Some effective thoughts for this:

____

____

____

____

You find that, for the moment, you are very worried about where your next penny is going to come from.

Some effective thoughts for this:

____

____

____

____

A waiter has given you very poor service. The main course was served without the vegetables, and everything took too long to arrive.

Some effective thoughts for this:

____

____

____

____

Your child has just failed a subject in school that you know full well he has the ability to pass with ease.

Some effective thoughts for this:

____

____

____

____

Your neighbour tells you with authority that your spouse has been having an affair.

Some effective thoughts for this:

____

____

____

____

Your new car was dented in the parking space and the offender is nowhere in sight.

Some effective thoughts for this:

____

____

____

____

How did you make out? It takes some practice and imagination to find or figure out an effective thought or two for a particular situation, but the effort will pay off.

SEVEN

Proactive thought choosing (Plan A)

Once you have a few effective thoughts ready to go, you still have to choose them. When appropriate, use free will (Plan A). Be an aggressive, proactive thought-chooser, not simply a thought-user or abuser, a *chooser*.

A thought for your files (*choose one*)

DEFECTIVE THOUGHT

Things in this world really make me nervous. I have a perfect right to be nervous considering the circumstances.

EFFECTIVE THOUGHT

If I ever get nervous, I say, 'You're making yourself nervous.' Then I say, 'Are you enjoying or valuing being nervous?' Then I usually answer, 'No, I am not enjoying being nervous.'

So then I say, 'Stop choosing thoughts that make you nervous and start choosing thoughts that make you calm.' Then I follow my instructions to the letter and end up very calm.

In order to get a better understanding of how the thought choosing process works, let's look at the Bodymind Theatre.

The Bodymind Theatre

The Bodymind Theatre replicates what goes on in your body and mind – and your resulting behaviour. Your thoughts and your feelings are on the inside. Your behaviour, that small part of you as a person that goes public, is on the outside.

Envision yourself as the owner of the Bodymind Theatre

Your mind and body are a theatre: a lecture hall with an audience; a podium, which only has room for one speaker at a time; and a large area backstage. Everything that takes place outside of this theatre of yours is the realm of behaviour and everything inside of the Bodymind Theatre includes:

1 your feelings,

2 all your thoughts and

3 the part of you that actually chooses the thoughts that produce your present feelings and behaviour. The part of you that does the choosing is called the programme director. This programme director part of you is of great importance.

Definitions

- **The Bodymind Theatre Owner** – that's you. You are the sole owner, pro tem, of your body and your mind.
- **The Bodymind Theatre** – houses all of your feelings and your thoughts, as well as the part of you that is the theatre's programme director.
- **The Hook** – is a thought-stopping and thought-choosing device that can be used by you as programme director any time that you want to put on or pull off a thought from the podium/stage.

- **The Podium/Stage** – this is the place in front of the audience where only one thought-speaker is permitted at any one time. It is a house rule, that the audience (composed entirely of (feelings) is compelled to listen to any thought-speaker that is permitted on the podium.
- **Programme Director** – the programme director is really you. (Actually, the programme director resides in the frontal lobe of your brain [the thought-choosing section]. As a programme director you are the 'thought-chooser for the Bodymind Theatre.) It is your job to produce an excellent 'uncommonly successful' life programme. You have absolute authority, in every case, to make the final decision as to what thought (backstage) can stay on the podium to speak to the theatre audience (your feelings).
- **Thought Speaker** – represents the one and only thought that is permitted to occupy the podium at any particular point in time. All feelings in the theatre will listen in awe to this speaker.

House Rule: only one Thought Speaker is allowed on the podium at any given time.

Diagram of the Bodymind Theatre

The Bodymind Theatre contains only thoughts, feelings and one programme director (*see overleaf*).

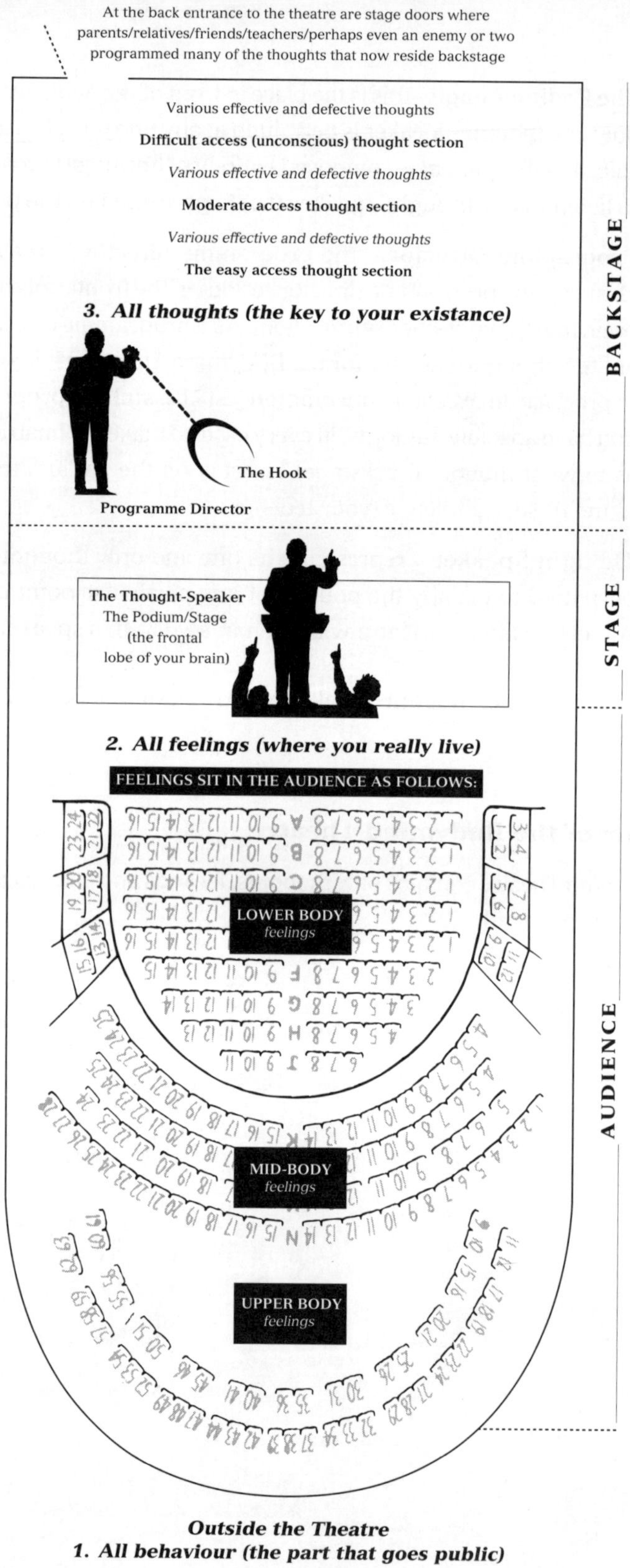

At the back entrance to the theatre are stage doors where parents/relatives/friends/teachers/perhaps even an enemy or two programmed many of the thoughts that now reside backstage
Various effective and defective thoughts
Difficult access (unconscious) thought section
Various effective and defective thoughts
Moderate access thought section
Various effective and defective thoughts
The easy access thought section
3. All thoughts (the key to your existance)
The Hook
Programme Director
BACKSTAGE
The Thought-Speaker
The Podium/Stage
(the frontal
lobe of your brain)
STAGE
2. All feelings (where you really live)
FEELINGS SIT IN THE AUDIENCE AS FOLLOWS:
LOWER BODY
feelings
MID-BODY
feelings
UPPER BODY
feelings
AUDIENCE
Outside the Theatre
1. All behaviour (the part that goes public)

YOU ARE THE PROGRAMME DIRECTOR

You, as the programme director, are 'the thought-chooser-in-chief.' The show that goes on in your mind is a product of the thoughts that you allow on the podium (the frontal lobe of your brain). Tell yourself, as programme director, to put on a show that is full and satisfying. After all, it is left up to you to choose effective thoughts instead of defective ones. Be a strong and decisive programme director. Use 'the hook' to pull any defective thought off the podium any time that you want to. If your natural mindset is working to your advantage (habits and conditioning) then nothing is required of you as programme director.

BE A STRONG PROGRAMME DIRECTOR

It is estimated that most people think to themselves a minimum of 100,000 words each day. That's a good-sized book, every day of our life. 365 books a year. Since this lecture series in your Bodymind Theatre will go on for your entire lifetime, see to it that the thoughts on your programme leads to the high quality of life that you owe to yourself.

Let defective thoughts rest in peace

If the thought turns out to be useful – then be sure to choose it frequently and if it is useless or defective, then be sure not to choose it. If a thought is defective, as programme director, permit it to remain backstage, never give it any privileges and let it die of attrition and neglect.

Your feelings are a captive audience

If the thought-speaker on the podium presents a useful and helpful thought (an effective thought), the audience of feelings will do very well, but if the thought-speaker on the podium presents a defective thought, your poor captive audience will feel and act accordingly. The audience of the Bodymind Theatre is composed of highly impressionable childlike feelings. Your feelings always follow the instructions of the thought speaker on the podium. Of course, it is you as programme director who has the final word as to which thought-speakers are permitted on the podium to speak to your feelings.

Your subconscious mind is backstage

Backstage are countless thoughts, some potentially effective, some defective, vying to get to the podium, but, according to the house rule (and biology) only one of these thoughts is permitted on stage in any given micro-second.

Many thoughts are vying to get on the podium

In your subconscious there are many, many potential speakers (thoughts) that want to get to the podium. Permit only **effective thought-speakers** to stay at the podium for any length of time. Sometimes, of course, it is difficult to differentiate an **effective thought-speaker** from a **defective thought-speaker**, but if you pause and identify effective thoughts, you will have little trouble.

Be on the lookout for new effective thoughts

There are, of course, some thoughts that try to bully their way on stage to take charge. Put these defective thoughts back in place. Let them die of inertia and disuse. Give that little effective thought over there in the corner a chance. You can make him a star. Be an effective thought 'star maker.' Have an effective thought talent hunt. Maybe there's an effective thought that no one ever heard of and you can make a discovery. Always keep your eye out for effective thought talent that you can someday use.

Often, **defective thought-speakers** try to disguise themselves as **effective thought-speakers**. These are pseudo-effective thoughts and are very dangerous. (For example, 'I **need** a relationship,' instead of 'I **prefer** a relationship,' etc.)

Take charge, produce a great show

Take out 'the hook' and pull him off stage. Be decisive. Replace him with that wonderful new effective thought that you have waiting in the wings. Of course, you must give yourself, as programme director, a chance to rest (sleeping at night) and then when that happens, of course, your thoughts will have free play. Dreaming keeps you sane. It is when you, as programme director, are resting that any thought that is strong enough can get on the podium. Fortunately, when we are dreaming, our feelings do not move out the door of the theatre and into action, unless, of course, we are sleep-walking.

Which programme director is the most effective?

One that says:

1. I'm afraid to run the show. I hope nice thoughts get on the podium. I can't do anything about it, if they don't.
2. Let's have fun. Any thought that wants, you're on.
3. Please do the show without me.
4. I just want it all to look good. You look like an effective thought, just from appearances alone. Why? I'll just choose you.

5 Those outside forces made me choose those thoughts.

6 My feelings made me choose that thought.

7 I was never in charge and I never will be in charge. I have no idea who is in charge. Who ever said I was in charge?

8 I am **definitely** in charge and I mean business. I am determined to programme a winning show. You, 'effective thought' over there. I'm putting you on the podium. Get ready to do a great job. Sorry 'defective thought' out there. Here's the hook. OK, 'effective thought', the spotlight is on you. Do your thing.

Obviously, the only programme director worth imitating on this list is **number 8**.

This programme director is wise and tough-minded and has many other qualities worth emulating when it come to running the theatre of your own mind.

The characteristics of the best programme director

- Knows when to take charge and when to rest.
- Gives sufficient rope, but is always capable of putting out the hook on a thought that proves defective
- Knows the difference between an effective thought and a defective one.
- Is loyal to the purposes of the Bodymind Theatre.
- Is determined to produce a programme that provides inner calm, a clear sense of purpose and plenty of adventure.
- Produces a programme that provides a great inner life, but not at the expense of any other person.

Exercising willpower

Relatively few individuals who promise themselves that they are going on a diet or are going to give up smoking or jog three miles every morning, do exactly what they say. New Year's resolutions fail in droves. Most of us just do not have sufficient resolve and staying power to keep our promises to ourselves. We mean well, but it becomes difficult to follow through. We mean to choose certain effective thoughts about dieting, exercise, confidence in our work and personal life, but then that resolve often fades. Truly successful people have more than average resolve and plenty of the required 'know-how' when it comes to the thought-choosing that they do. They have actually learned to have greater willpower, even when it was not their natural disposition. It is important to appreciate that 'greater willpower' can actually be learned, even if willpower was not one of your natural talents when you started out in life.

A thought for your files (*choose one*)

DEFECTIVE THOUGHT

I'm a positive thinker. I look on the bright side – always.

EFFECTIVE THOUGHT

I'm a realistic positive thinker. I face the facts as they are and work upward from there.

Visualisation

We think with pictures as well as with words. Visualise yourself successfully dealing with any condition that is giving you trouble. Suppose, for example, that you have a very abrasive type of boss and that when this boss of yours is in your vicinity, you become extremely nervous and foul up your work. The issue then would be to overcome your nervousness when the boss is around. Shut your eyes and imagine your boss peering over your shoulder while you are trying to work. When you can actually feel yourself getting upset and nervous, signal that fact to yourself by extending your forefinger. This will take a moment or two, then open your eyes and relax your hands and rest a bit.

Then shut your eyes again, but this time imagine your boss peering over your shoulder without your getting nervous at all. This will probably take a bit longer to do than the first step, but when you can successfully picture this happening, open your eyes. Then reflect on what it was you were thinking when you did not become nervous, even though your boss was over your shoulder. Were you ignoring him? Were you thinking that he/she was silly or unimportant? Or were simply concentrating entirely on the job in front of you, and no one else, not even your boss. Whatever it was that you were thinking in the second instance can serve as an effective thought to choose whenever the event actually happens, whenever your boss actually does look over your shoulder. Practise using effective visualisations for any disturbing factor. Then, when an actual circumstance occurs, you will have some effective thoughts ready that you can consciously choose.

Helping yourself

It is necessary to practising effective thought-choosing. Here's how to motivate yourself to practise.

Exercise

List below a few activities that you enjoy, that give you pleasure.

(Ideas: enjoying TV, playing a certain sport, eating certain desserts, speaking to someone special on the phone, etc.)

____

____

____

Below, list a few activities that you find onerous, things you do not enjoy.

(For example, cleaning the house, working on your budget, calling your in-laws, etc.)

____

____

____

Now, make a deal with yourself using the activities that you like to do as rewards and the things you find onerous as punishments

Put your contract with yourself in writing.

I, ______________________________________ (YOUR NAME)

promise to practice effective thought-choosing, regularly. If I do, I will receive the following rewards: *Write several rewards below*:

____

____

____

If I do not practice, I will penalise myself as follows:

Write the penalty below:

____

____

____

Systematically practise effective thought-choosing a number of times every day. Reward yourself if you practise, by treating yourself to some of your favourite activities: going for walks, going to the theatre or a film, going to a match, playing golf, or having a hot bath. If you don't do your practise, penalise yourself by cleaning the house, preparing tax returns, balancing the books, mowing the lawn, cooking, doing push-ups, etc. What is a reward or a penalty is best known to you.

Rewarding and penalising yourself is a sound and proven way for shaping your own effective thinking behaviour. Of course, the best reward is the effective feelings and action that will result from the effective thoughts that you actively choose.

A thought for your files (*choose one*)

DEFECTIVE THOUGHT

I'm not really responsible for myself. Outside circumstances make me act in certain ways.

EFFECTIVE THOUGHT

The one thing that I truly own is me. I accept and enjoy taking full responsibility for myself.

A PERSONAL EXAMPLE

One evening recently, I was driving for over three hours to give a talk to a business group. 'Oh boy, am I tired,' I thought to myself, as I stared bleary-eyed over the steering wheel. I could hardly manage to keep my eyes open, yet I knew that within the next half hour I would be facing a large audience of professionals. Besides, driving while feeling so tired is dangerous. Then I reminded myself that I wasn't really tired, but rather my thoughts were making me tired. This didn't ring true to me at first. 'Who are you kidding? I'm really tired. I have every right to be tired. Up late last night. Working hard.' The whole routine, but then the wiser part of myself persisted. 'No, it's your thoughts that are making you tired. You know that's the case. Now's the time to put what you know, what you preach, into practice.' I then said to myself, rather dryly at first, 'You're choosing thoughts that are making you tired. That's right, tired thoughts.' I allowed that admission to penetrate the defences that are so often mounted against taking personal responsibility for one's own thoughts and feelings. It took a few moments, but the reality of what I was saying to myself eventually penetrated. I then began to think wake-up thoughts, mischievous, thoughts. These thoughts definitely made me feel brighter, perhaps, a little too much and I arrived at the lecture hall full of pep and energy. Why not be energetic and effective, instead of deservedly tired and ineffective?

EIGHT

Pausing to win

The main purpose for pausing is to break self-defeating mindsets. As an effective thinker, you must pause whenever you happen to notice that you are not moving relentlessly toward the highly satisfying life that I presume you have set your sights on. If you have a 'mindset problem,' pause to turn that problem into a 'mindset solution.'

We have all been 'hypnotised'

In effect, all minds (including yours) are 'programmed' with a wide variety of thoughts, beginning from day one, after birth. If what is lurking in our subconscious mindsets is working on our behalf, it makes sense not to tamper with it. But if our mindsets are in any way working against our best interests (preventing us, for example, from becoming fully successful) then it makes sense to break that mindset and replace it with a more effective one.

If you have ever passed your turning place whilst driving, you were in a hypnotic trance.

One time recently, I was entranced with my own thoughts, driving cross country to conduct a seminar. My mind must have been a million miles away, for, suddenly, I found myself at a toll booth with the toll collector peering into my window. I opened the window, and, I'm sure as a matter of conditioning and habit, I found myself saying, 'OK, fill it up.'

Have you ever gone to a film and become so fascinated that you didn't know what happened to the time. You were in a bit of a hypnotic trance. The same happens when you read a good book.

Try this experiment. Fold your arms as you might usually do. Now unfold them. Now fold them together again, but this time, try placing the arm that was below the other, over the top. You can do that of course, but it probably feels very strange, because it is not your habitual way.

If, as you are reading this, you're in a position to cross your legs, please do so, in your customary fashion. Now, uncross your legs. Now cross them again, but this time, place the opposite leg on top of the other. It probably feels a bit strange and it should. After all, you have been crossing your legs habitually the same way for many years.

There is the story of the woman who looked at herself in her bedroom mirror every night before going to bed. One night, they had guests coming for dinner and she went up to her bedroom to get dressed for dinner. Out of habit, she took one look at herself in her bedroom mirror. Got undressed and went to bed. Her husband found her fast asleep when he went upstairs to tell her that the guests had arrived.

Breaking a self-defeating mindset

Sometimes, during seminars, I ask 'How many of you are familiar with Ivan Pavlov's concept of the conditioned response.' Almost without fail, there are always a number of persons in the audience that automatically raise their hands. Raising hands is something we learned as little children in school. It is a matter of habit. Then I ask, 'Who asked you to raise your hand?' Most persons who have raised their hands smile sheepishly, recognising how their conditioning caused them to respond – a kind of mass hypnosis. To demonstrate the way to break any mindset through pausing, I later ask the same audience, once again, the same question: 'How many of you are familiar with Ivan Pavlov's concept of the conditioned response?' This time no hands go up. Why?

That occurs, of course, because during the pause, rethinking takes place permitting the individual to break the mindset, the habit, the conditioning that caused them to automatically raise their hand. The audience member thinks to himself, 'If you think that you're going to catch me on your crafty little trick twice, think again. I'm not going to fall for it.'

Prompts for pausing

One of the most obvious cues is to simply say to yourself 'Stop.' You probably would do best to say this silently to yourself, but even out loud can help, if need be. Use some kind of wording that will command your full attention. Some of my clients tell me that they use 'detach, detach, detach.' They say that that reminds them to detach themselves momentarily, at least, from the situation or person that is upsetting them. 'You're getting yourself all upset,' they often say to themselves. 'Stop what you are thinking and take time out.'

The remedy that our parents used and taught us serves the very same purpose. 'Hold your breath and count to ten!' In some schools they have a special room for disruptive students to calm down. Go to your own special room.

In your imagination, take a helicopter trip out of the situation so that you can be detached from it and see it with greater perspective.

Other people 'pause' by stepping out of their environment to go to the toilet, in the US sometimes quite aptly called 'the rest room.' Even just taking a long, deep breath can be the signal to yourself to pause. Pinch yourself. Remind yourself in any way you can to remove yourself mentally from your present situation, stop action and calm down. Whenever you are functioning off target, pause for as long as necessary to do some genuine problem solving.

Perhaps you already have a favourite trigger action to help you take time out. This action, the rubbing of your hip, the unbuttoning of your collar, the loosening of your tie, or whatever, should be a clear signal to yourself to pause. Even kicking yourself can do the job. Do whatever works for you. Just make certain to pause in terms of whatever you find upsetting or getting in the way of your full and satisfying life objective.

The length of pause

Once you have paused, you have some very important 'detective work' to do. Why have you permitted yourself to get sufficiently upset to take you off course from your main goal – a great life? It is sometimes necessary to pause for only a moment if you have plenty of experience in handling the situation you face. Of course, some problems will require that you pause for quite a long time, sometimes months, if the issue that you are facing is very complex and very deep.

Pausing can be in the form of a week's holiday, a sabbatical leave, a mind journey of a few minutes, or a thought that passes by in a flash. Pausing is what the successful high diver does on the spring board in a microsecond just before he takes off on a double jack knife. It is what the golfer does who has unfortunately 'double bogeyed' the previous hole.

Life goes on even during the pause

Remember, however, all other aspects of your life will still go on as before. You must learn to compartmentalise and pause regarding one segment of your life, and keep all the rest going on – business as usual. When you are pausing, other aspects of your life do not come to a halt. During the pause, while you are doing your effective thinking detective work (identifying the culprit defective thoughts and identifying or creating the necessary effective thoughts to replace them), your external life still goes on. There's work that needs to be done, bills to be paid, meetings to attend and prepare for, children to watch over, etc. Life still goes on. You can still keep typing, or filing, or walking and even talking, in tandem with pausing over the issue that is giving you trouble.

So in actuality, be clear that you are only pausing in regard to the issue (or issues) that you are facing, but that doesn't mean that the rest of your life goes on hold as well.

PAULA THOMPSON LOSES A BIG SALE

Paula Thompson, a 39 year old computer software sales engineer, loses out on making that big sale which she had expected to close. She is temporarily devastated. But she still continues to make more sales calls. At the same time that she is making productive sales calls, Paula is also busy figuring out what she might have done differently with regard to the lost sale, so that she won't make the same mistake again.

RALPH PAUSES TO TOLERATE

Ralph Larkin, a 37 year old project director, uses pausing as a logical way to help him tolerate the many abrasive (and unnecessary) memos that his boss, Paul Strain keeps sending him. He is required to respond in writing to each of these memos, because, in his company, memo writing is a long standing ritual. He pauses to break his 'normal' response pattern of getting upset by Paul Strain's latest memo.

'I say to myself, 'stop, stop.' I catch myself. I take a deep breath and I calm down, and pause to rethink. Whenever I receive one of those foolish memos from my boss, Paul, I say to myself, 'Wait a minute, Ralph, you weren't put on this planet to get upset. After all, you have a commitment to enjoy what you have left of your life to the hilt.' It seems that my idiot boss's memo writing is part and parcel of that short life that I'm determined to enjoy. What can I do about it? Well, I make it my business to stop whenever I get one of those blasted things and I've learned to laugh like hell to myself. I see it as funny. Stupid, time wasting, but funny. I've come to realise that enjoying life takes some doing, especially around here.'

During the pause, Ralph reminds himself that no one need know what he's thinking. That's his private business, business that takes place most effectively after pausing and breaking his mindset.'

Ralph has learned how to keep a straight face and laugh to himself while 'pausing.' He breaks his suffering mindset and chooses worthwhile thoughts to keep him from getting overly upset with a work condition which is out of his own full control.

A new mindset

The ant doesn't know it is in an ant hole

MARSHALL MCLUHAN

Marshall McLuhan author of *The Medium is the Message*, said that the ant in the ant hole doesn't realise that it is in an ant hole while it is in there. Then one day, the ant crawls out of its ant hole and looks down and says, 'My goodness. Look where I was. It's hard to believe that I've been spending so much of my life down there.' It is then, and only then, outside the ant hole and peering down, that it really sees where it was. An entirely new mindset. A new vantage point. If that very same ant, one day, while crawling around in what it has come to think of as the 'real' world crawls up a glass wall and then finds that it is a glass enclosure on top of Houston's astrodome, it will get another new perspective, look down and say, 'Oh, that's where I have been – in an astrodome.' The point is that a new perspective provides a more complete picture and greater wisdom.

Mindset exercises

In order for you to better appreciate how easy it is to be victimised, even when warned, by a self-defeating mindset, try each of the following exercises. I think the value of pausing to break your mindset will become very clear to you after you try these exercises. During your short 'pause,' try to see if there is an alternative way of looking at the exercise that will lead to an easy solution. Always reserve the right to look at any situation any way that you want to. We all have this capacity. I call this capacity, the capacity to have 'optional illusions'.

> **Warning**
>
> Each of the following exercises deliberately tries to mislead you. So be sure to pause and then during that pause, be sure to do some unconventional (yet effective) thinking so you can easily solve each exercise.

Exercise 1: The nine dots

Try to connect the following nine dots with only four straight, continuous lines, without lifting your pencil off the paper. If you haven't done this exercise before please give it a try and then look on the next page for the answer. Hint: try a new perspective. Your mindset is probably suggesting that you start by staying within the boundaries of the nine dots. Be sure to pause, break any conventional mindset you have, and then look at the bigger picture if you want to solve this problem (*see over*).

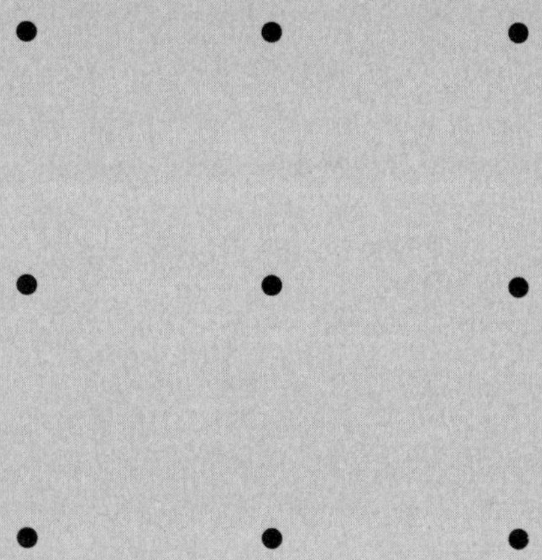

Exercise 2: The mop, cop, hop routine

Answer these questions as rapidly as possible.

- In order to wipe water up from the floor, one might use a ______________

  (The answer, of course is – MOP)

- What does a rabbit do when it moves? ______________

  (The answer is 'HOP')

- Another name for a policeman that begins with a 'C'? ______________

  (The answer is, of course – COP)

- What is the first thing you do when you come to a green light? ______________

  (Be sure to pause before giving your answer.)

Exercise 3: The capital gimmick

How do you pronounce the capital of Switzerland? Gen-ev-a or Gen – eva? (Pause, and then during the pause watch out that you have not been entrapped by the way that the question has been phrased.)

Answers:

1 The nine dots are connected as follows: (Note that the starting point is beyond the normal boundary that most persons who do not pause will use.)

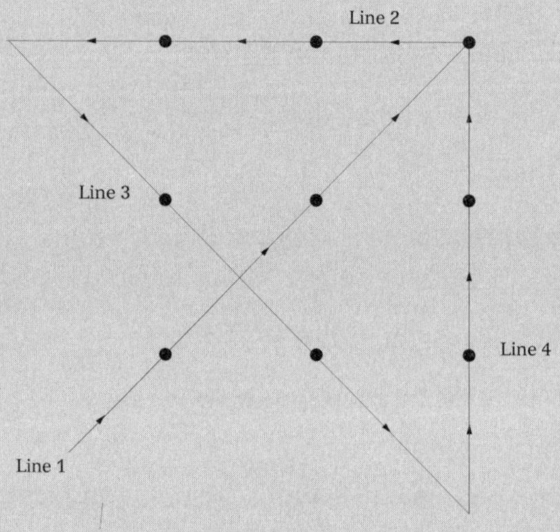

2 The answer for the last question is, of course, 'go,' not 'stop.' (If you did not pause, then out of conditioning and rhyming, you may have found yourself quickly saying 'stop.' It is of course not only foolish, but sometimes even dangerous to stop at a green light.)

3 The capital of Switzerland is Berne, not Geneva.

Pause and win

By breaking a self-defeating mindset by pausing, you can then install a more effective mindset and win. Remember, when things get tough, pause and choose.

NINE

Subconscious strategies (Plan B)

Effective thinkers first try to proactively choose thoughts at the conscious level. That's always their Plan A, but if their social and/or genetic programming is getting in the way of their proactive, conscious thought choosing, here are some subconscious tactics (Plan B) that they use to help them to choose effective thoughts.

Some Plan Bs

Plan Bs provide a means for reprogramming your subconscious where many defective thoughts reside.

Dealing with a 'runaway' feeling

One aspect of Plan B is to make things better by first making things worse. Sometime or another you might feel that an emotion is running away with you, and you find that fighting it directly proves useless. For example, did you ever feel depressed, but for no clear reason? Then did you try to pep yourself up and find that the more you tried to feel better, the worse you began to feel?

You can usually lift your 'downer' feelings by not trying so hard. That is, you merely apply a very powerful method called the go-along technique, a technique I informally refer to as 'The Cowboy Technique'.

Picture in your mind The Cowboy in one of those old time cowboy movies. He is, of course, riding a beautiful horse and wearing a big white hat. Suddenly a passing stagecoach comes by, its horses totally out of control. The passengers scream for help and there's The Cowboy to the rescue. He brings his mount alongside the stagecoach and leaps bravely onto it. The horses and stagecoach are obviously far out of control, but The Cowboy does not falter. He gets to the front, climbs over the wild horses, and grasps the reins. The Cowboy, now fully asserting control, does not stop, but rides the horses **another** mile or so down the road, affirming that he is in control of the wild horses. The horses begin to sense that someone is holding the reins and they slow down. After a short period of time, he looks over to the admiring passengers and says, 'Whooah,' to the horses, bringing them to a full stop. The Cowboy turns the now docile horses in another direction, the direction of The Cowboy's choice. The background music becomes gentle as The Cowboy leads the stagecoach through town.

Our hero offers an important lesson here. Imagine that your thoughts are running wild in a particular mindset, as did the horse-drawn stagecoach. (Your thoughts might run wild into depression, disenchantment, anger, fear, any number of counterproductive directions.) The Cowboy did something very intelligent and natural in this little scenario that we rarely choose to do when we are trying to catch a runaway series of thoughts. He went along with what was already going on. Then, when eventually he found the reins of the wild horses, he rode with them in *the direction that they were going* for a short time. He asserted to them that he was in charge – even though they were off and running. It became impossible for the poor horses to sense whether they were still in command or if The Cowboy was. The Cowboy made certain that the horses knew that it was he who held the reins. After he sensed that they were fully aware that he was in charge, he pulled them to a halt. Only then did he turn them in the direction that he wished to go off into the town. Once you have shown your runaway thoughts that it is you in charge of them, it is within your power to take your thoughts and feelings where you choose.

LIZA'S STRATEGY

A 52 year old widow, Liza, told me how angry her 21 year old daughter Ann, made her feel. Liza had raised her daughter on her own with great personal sacrifice. Her husband died when their daughter was only three. Working overtime countless hours as a secretary, she saw to it that Ann could afford to go on to university. Then in her first year, Ann, without the slightest consultation with her mother, quit university and ran off 'to live with a dreadful, unemployed musician,' as Liza put it. 'I have a perfect right to be angry, don't I?' she asked, seeking reassurance. 'After all that I've sacrificed, look how little I have to show for it.'

Liza told me how she learned to take personal responsibility for her plight and eventually, to turn her unhappy situation around.

Although she continued to believe that her daughter's behaviour was abominable and unjust, she managed to come to grips with the reality that there was absolutely nothing she could do about it, for the time being. She appreciated that there was nothing to be gained by remaining in a constant state of anger. Here is how Liza proceeded to link up with her anger-producing thoughts, take full command, and turn to a more effective kind of thinking. When she first realised how angry she was, she acknowledged the fact, 'I am very angry. I'm not just angry, I'm furious.' Then she said (in her mind's eye, of course), 'I'm choosing thoughts that are making me angry.' These words almost stuck in her throat. It was difficult, naturally, for Liza to admit that it was her thoughts and not her daughter's behaviour that made her feel so angry. After all, she had more than 50 years of previous conditioning and training in blaming outside conditions for what she was feeling inside. However, she eventually did manage to link up with her anger-producing mindset. Then she carried her anger as far as she wanted to. 'Let's see,' she thought, 'let me try to make my stomach get tight.' That thought helped, and her stomach got a bit tighter than it already was. Then she tried to think a thought or two that would make her clench her fists more and tighten up her jaw. Again she met with some success, demonstrating to her previously out-of-control anger-producing thoughts that she was firmly in control. After a while she had had enough of anger and decided to think thoughts that would make her calm. She chose some thoughts about yellow flowers in a beautiful green field that she had stored in her memory. Slowly, her pulse returned to normal. The flow of angry adrenaline came to a stop. Liza took off, in her mind's eye, into the sunset, past the yellow flowers, and over the beautiful green hill. Liza had successfully linked up with her undesirable thoughts; she took command and turned her emotional state completely around. Of course, she still had a lot of unresolved business with her daughter – but that she was able to 'work-through' later at her own pace.

One might ask, 'Isn't such control a form of repression? Won't that anger come out somewhere else? Won't Liza, for example, find it necessary to kick the dog when she gets home – just to let this buried anger out?' The answer to this query is a resounding 'No'.

This is not repression at all. Liza fully acknowledged her angry thoughts. She did not repress her anger. She rode with this emotion for a while, took command of the feeling, took responsibility for the thoughts that were producing the feeling, and simply chose other, more effective, thoughts – which produced more effective (less angry) feelings.

Still, you might be wondering, what about when Liza's mind drifts back to thoughts of her daughter living with that despicable musician? Won't those thoughts make her just as angry as before? After all, her daughter was not very sensitive to her mother's feelings or respectful of her mother's wishes and Liza did apparently sacrifice a great deal for her daughter's university education, did she not?

Of course, I agree that if Liza returns to thinking about herself as self-sacrificing or betrayed, she is bound to get angry. However, over a period of time, she developed more effective (and much more realistic) attitudes toward her daughter's dropping out of college and living with someone without being married, which were but a few ideas that were upsetting to her. There are, of course, a variety of ways of looking at many of the issues that life presents. For example, who ever said, 'You can rely on your children to respect you'? That may be nice, but it is not a self-managing concept, as you will come to see.

The point is, that if one does not choose the thoughts that produce anger or any other emotion, then such an emotion does not come into being. Therefore, no emotion is being repressed. So, by choosing your thoughts intelligently, you can greatly reduce, if not eliminate, any unwanted emotional condition, be it fear, worry, guilt, tension, etc.

Sometimes, it is difficult to deal with a feeling when you are unable to identify the particular thoughts causing such a feeling.

CLIVE'S MALAISE

> A few years ago, Clive, a successful surgeon, came to me for counselling, complaining of a generalised feeling of anxiety. 'I get very depressed all of a sudden, and I don't seem to be able to put my finger on just why. I get this horrible low feeling that just comes on me out of the blue, and I don't know what to do about it. It seems to come for no apparent reason, even when everything in my life is going well. I have almost everything I always wanted. Materially, we're blessed. My wife is loving and caring. Our children are terrific. Why do I get this way? What can I do about it?'

My recommendation to him was identical to that which we have been discussing. In essence: 'Go along with the feeling for a while. Don't try so hard to fight it – or to figure out what's causing it. Choose thoughts that will make you even more depressed. Make yourself sad by thinking of all the things others have that you don't have. Make yourself cry a little because you are not appreciated by everyone. Identify in yourself something that can make you feel down, and then choose thoughts that will bring you down even further. By doing this, you will be taking charge of your feelings. Then, after a reasonable period of time (*the shorter the better*) ask yourself, 'Is this the way I want to continue to feel?' Then if your answer is no, choose thoughts that take you into a different emotional state. It's easier done than said, so start taking charge of your feeling states now.

What seemed to be adding to Clive's anxiety was the fear that he was out of control. By going along with and then deepening his depression, he enabled himself to get a handle on what was at first out of his reach.

Sometimes, of course, because of years of family conditioning, some people do learn to **repress** their emotions, leading to a wooden existence. In those instances, it becomes necessary to permit oneself to feel more deeply – even such emotions as anger or hate can be valuable.

TED'S FEELINGS

Ted and Elaine, a couple having marital difficulties, came to me for counselling. Elaine's complaint centred on Ted's 'lack of emotion, lack of being able to express feelings.' 'He's so damn nice about everything that it makes me sick. I only wish that he would get angry once in a while. But no. All he ever does is smile and be nice. I can't stand it anymore.'

Ted wanted to be more expressive, he said, 'But what can I do about it?' Eventually he figured out that he, alone, would have to take responsibility for his lack of emotional expression. By choosing thoughts, quite deliberately, to make himself angry and by also choosing thoughts that said, 'It's okay to express such feelings sometimes; it might even help my relationship with Elaine,' Ted learned to become more expressive.

Going along with, and then taking charge of, any undesired emotion is an extremely effective tool that you must remind yourself to employ. Moreover, you must remind yourself that even though life might sometimes treat you unfairly, there is still much that you can do to at least lessen the damage. Which brings us to the next powerful concept.

Using 90 second, rapid self-hypnosis

Another possible Plan B for subconscious thought-choosing is that of rapid self-hypnosis. The conscious mind is, on the outside, a relatively thin layer that protects your subconscious. Your conscious mind is a bit sceptical of certain ideas, especially if they are not particularly reasonable. Your subconscious mind isn't very sceptical at all. It is, in fact, quite naive. Your naive subconscious has a tendency to accept practically anything that gets into it. If what gets into it is effective, that, of course, is marvellous, but if what gets into the subconscious is working against your best interests, then that, of course, is a different story.

ACCESS TO YOUR OWN SUBCONSCIOUS

The vast majority of our thoughts is housed in our subconscious. The subconscious mind is programmed during the first five or six years of one's life. That's why spending time with one's children during their formative years is so important.

Dr W Penfield, a noted neurosurgeon, reported in 1959 that our mind is very much like a tape recorder. Through electrical stimulation of the brain, during a brain surgery, Penfield found that we have actually recorded in our brains literally every perception that we have ever had. In your mind is a recording of the food your mother was cooking in the kitchen and what it smelled like, while you were still crawling around on the living room floor, taking it all in, subconsciously.

Unfortunately, access to your own subconscious is not all that easy once you move past age six. Consciously repeating an effective thought to yourself over and over again sometimes doesn't work and the reason for that is quite uncomplicated. The programme in your subconscious mind is rejecting the thought that you are trying to choose and sending other thoughts up to the foreground of your conscious mind in its place. How, then, do you quell your subconscious mind and reprogramme it?

Damaging subconscious thoughts

There are, for example, many attractive people walking around right now who think that they are quite ugly and that is only because that message got into their subconscious when they were a child and is still working (quite negatively) against them. These people don't even see their own beauty when they see themselves in the mirror – they reject compliments. All because of their programming.

Hypnosis has been misunderstood because it has been so abusively handled by charlatans and stage hypnotists for so many years. No one need be made to feel foolish or embarrassed by using this technique. There is absolutely nothing magical or secret about it. I deliberately avoid using the misnomer 'hypnosis' as much as possible, because the prefix hypno is derived from the Greek word that means sleep, but you are never really asleep when you employ this technique. Rather, you are preoccupied with your imagination, you are entranced! Actually, it is more like the condition you are in just before you fall asleep each night.

Undoubtedly, you have been entranced on many occasions: while driving past your motorway exit, watching a good film, reading an interesting book, staring at the TV, or even sitting in a classroom. Your power of imagination, your capacity for creative self-deception and the ability to make suggestions to yourself are all fully utilised when you engage in the technique of auto-suggestion.

Through the self-hypnosis technique (Plan B), you are able to rest your conscious mind and speak directly to your subconscious. All that is involved is that you 'reprogramme' your subconscious and tell it in no uncertain terms, in essence, 'Please keep quiet, you useless, **self-sabotaging** defective thought!'

90 second rapid self-hypnosis is a tactic that I have successfully taught to many of my clients. Once you have identified an effective thought or two that you would like to inject into your subconscious, then you can always use this method to assist you in thought-choosing. 90-second rapid self-hypnosis gives your free-will thought-choosing a subconscious boost. As you know, direct access to your own subconscious becomes increasingly difficult as we get older. That's why a small child's subconscious is easier to 'programme' than that of an adult.

The way to get past the protection of your conscious (sometimes overly sceptical) mind is to temporarily confuse and baffle it, stun it and get it out of operation, and then quickly blag any effective thoughts, that you have prepared in advance for yourself – past it and right into the naive subconscious. Your conscious mind is really just a thin covering (but tough to penetrate) that covers the largest portion of your mind which is, of course, subconscious. Below is an illustration:

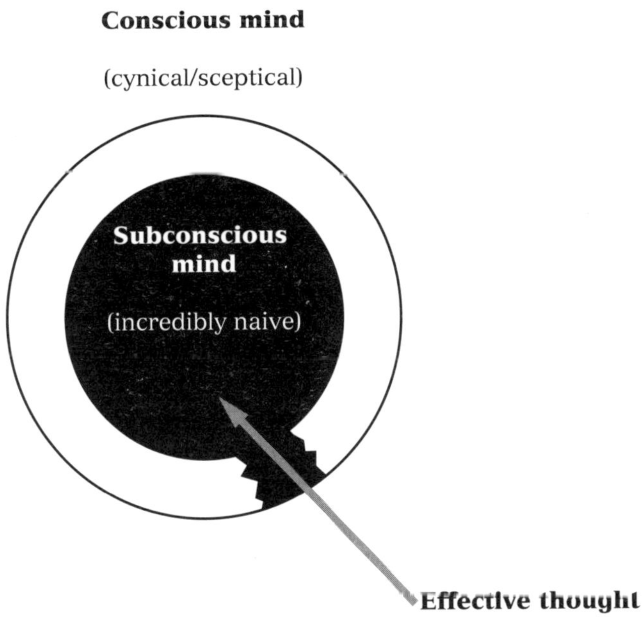

Effective thought (prepared in advance)

The first step is to relax the conscious mind, before you divert it. The second step is to confuse and divert it by using a process called creative self-deception. The third step is to enter the effective thought directly into your subconscious while the conscious mind is diverted. And the fourth is a move back into consciousness, with your subconscious now safely reprogrammed.

In advance of using rapid self-hypnosis, it is necessary to prepare the effective thought that you wish to choose. Once you have your effective thought ready, follow this four step process:

1 Say to yourself *'green one – relax'*

The first step in rapid self-hypnosis is to relax the conscious mind. Simply take a deep breath, make your forehead very tight and then relax it. That is all that you have to do at this phase. You do not have to be in the proverbial deep, mysterious hypnotic trance. Levels of trance can be measured from level 1 (very slight) to 5 (deep). You only have to be at level 1 for rapid self-hypnosis to take effect. After you have relaxed just a bit, say the word 'enter' to yourself. Think of the word 'enter' as being very much like the enter button on the computer. It enters that thought (relax) into your mental programming.

The next step involves creative self-deception, a concept that we discussed earlier, so that you can get past the cynical conscious mind that is guarding your naive subconscious.

2 Then say to yourself *'green two – I can't separate my two fingers'*

Here you hold you thumb and forefinger together and say to yourself, 'No matter how hard I try, I cannot separate my two fingers.' Then try very hard to separate them but *don't do it.* If you do separate them, you will have won the battle, but have lost the war. This is when creative self-deception comes into play. Your sceptical conscious mind will be telling you, 'Nonsense. You can separate your fingers.' Don't listen at all to your sceptical conscious mind. You aim is to confuse it and bypass it. So listen to your wiser self (the uncommonly successful side of your personality) and do not separate your fingers. Then say (for the second time) 'green.' That's excellent use of creative self-deception, and now at this point you have direct access to your hard to get at subconscious.

3 Then at *green three – repeat the effective thought to yourself*

The third step, now that you have direct access to your own subconscious, is to inject the effective thought that you have prepared in advance into your own subconscious. I recommend repeating it to yourself three times, each time, getting more and more forceful about it. You can also, at this point, tell any defective thoughts that you may have identified to remain quiet and take a back seat, because you are just not going to use them.'

4 Finally at *green four* say to yourself *'Separate fingers, wake up – reprogrammed'*

And lastly, now that your subconscious has been reprogrammed with the effective thought or thoughts that you prepared, you simply *separate your fingers* and say to yourself – 'OK, I'm reprogrammed now. Enter.' And then with your fingers fully functioning now, do enter the real world with your subconscious now effectively reprogrammed. You should know that this 'reprogramming' can be expected to last about 14 hours, and then it becomes necessary to do it again, until the effective thoughts that you put in there this way really take root. It is also possible to do this several times each day, that is if it is practical for you.

Let's take you through a real situation that you currently are facing and, step-by-step, use the rapid self-hypnosis method to help you deal with it.

Exercise: Practice, practice, practice

Using your own shorthand, write down a reminder of an issue (personal or professional) that you are facing that involves effective thinking. It can be a major issue or minor one. Perhaps it involves your working environment, getting along with someone in your job, your boss, a colleague or a friend. Or it can be a personal issue such as being overweight, or smoking, or worrying about your children, spouse, or parents.

An issue that is currently giving me some aggravation:

____

____

____

What are one or more effective thoughts that you believe will help you with this issue?

____

____

____

Now that you have identified one or more effective thoughts that you would like to choose, let us once again go step by step through the 90-second rapid self-hypnosis method, but this time actually try out each step until you become proficient at it.

Self hypnosis

Green one: Say to yourself 'Relax'

Green two: Say to yourself 'Can't separate my fingers.'

(Then try to separate your fingers but don't succeed, or you will have 'won the battle but lost the war.')

Green three: Repeat the effective thought that you identified above – three times, each time saying the effective thought in stronger and stronger terms.

Green four: Say to yourself, 'OK, now, I can separate my fingers. (do so). Then say to yourself: 'Wake up, reprogrammed.'

That's it, for at least the next 14 hours. You've given yourself a tool for choosing. You still must exercise willpower regarding that thought as well, but now, at least, you've stacked the odds for your thought-choosing success very much in your own favour.

Tricks for your imagination

Imagination is the process whereby you actually see an image or picture in your mind's eye without necessarily having the stimulus for the image in your actual physical vicinity. Interestingly, if you imagine something happening vividly enough, your body and nervous system will react just as if that which you are imagining is actually taking place. It is surprising how easy it is to trick your whole body and entire nervous system by using the powers of imagination. For example, if you were to imagine that a shadow behind a curtain is really the figure of an intruder, your hand might actually begin to sweat, your mouth get dry, your heart rate quicken. A person's body and nervous system reacts in exactly the same way whether it is really an intruder, a friend, disguised as an intruder, playing a poor practical joke, or merely a shadow from the tree outside.

It is not that our nervous systems and bodies are stupid. It is merely that figuring out whether our thoughts are right or wrong is not the job of our nerves and body. That is the job of our mind. Consequently, our imagination can be employed as either a very good friend or a very poor one. Why not, then, make your own imagination a very good friend?

You must use your imagination to 'get past' your conscious mind and speak directly to your subconscious. Your conscious mind is much more orderly and logical than your subconscious mind. The former is usually sceptical about outside suggestions, and scepticism is generally a pretty good idea, but in order to reprogramme your subconscious mind, you must get past this cautious gatekeeper. This is where the use of creative, temporary self-deception comes into play.

Here is how you employ creative self-deception. Put the conscious, logical, sceptical part of your mind to rest. That is, gain your conscious mind's confidence, and then surreptitiously slip the effective new thought (that you've planned in advance) past it while it is looking the other way. Treat your subconscious mind to more effective new thoughts regularly in this manner. A person's subconscious is extremely trusting and naive. That's why the conscious part of you is so protective. Once something gets past the conscious gatekeeper, the subconscious gobbles up, quite indiscriminately, this new data. In this instance, of course, you are going to feed only thoughts that are very effective. It is difficult, if not impossible, to tell what has slipped into your subconscious over your lifetime, but that matters little once you have in your hands an effective means to reprogramme yourself properly.

TEN

Accessing your hidden identity

Who are you?

Effective thinkers definitely know who they are. Most other people do not really know who they are.

I am going to try to make you clarify your real identity by asking you, in a variety of ways, 'Who are you?' Each time that I ask the question, I will vary the emphasis just a bit. Your job is to give a different answer each time. I'll start with your name. Please write it down. Then I'll move on to job and family. Then beyond that. I think that you will find out something very interesting about your real identity as you go through this exercise.

Exercise

Who are you? (answer with your name, please)

Answer: I am ________________________________

Who are you *really*? (this time answer with your job title)

Answer: I am ________________________________

That's what you do, but who are you? (now answer with one or more of your family roles – a mother, father, husband, wife, sister, son, daughter etc.)

Answer: I am ________________________________

But that is not *who* you are either. That's just a role. A function. *Who* are you, please? (now, say, me.)

Answer: I am ______________________________

Of course, you are you. But that doesn't say anything. Who are '*you*?' You are certainly more than just a 'me'. (Now answer the question any way that you would like, but differently from any answer that you gave before.)

Answer: I am ______________________________

Yes, I know what you said, but who is the *real* you? (answer differently again, in your own way.)

Answer: I am ______________________________

Yes, of course. *But who are you*?

Answer: I am ______________________________

Sure. *But who are you*?

Answer: I am ______________________________

You, of all people, should definitely know who you are. If you don't, who does? If you don't define yourself, who will? There are plenty of people, I'm sure, who might define you, but on their terms and not yours.

Most people who go through with this exercise are left with an uneasy feeling. Unfortunately, most of us do not have a very clear picture of who we really are. We often get their identity from organisations or groups, but effective thinkers are selective joiners, and they never get their primary sense of identity from that which they join. They get their primary sense of identity from their own inner self-picture.

Certainly, who we are is not just our given name.

Your name, of course, is just a conditioned response. If your name is called you will notice an almost automatic response. That's not who you are. Your name is just a convenient handle, a tag.

Of course our name is quite important to us, as is our job title and our family role, but these are conditioned responses or roles and not who we really are. Job title and the fact that you are father, mother, brother, etc are really roles and/or functions that you want to do well by. These labels are not your true identity. Your true identity is a much deeper issue than a simple label, role or function. We all have an outer image and that image plays a major role in managing others, but it is your inner image, the picture you have about your self, that is central to self management.

Philosophers, theologians, and psychologists all agree on one thing: there is absolutely no agreement on the fundamental nature of human beings: no one really knows whether they are inherently good or evil, or even if they are free or controlled.

To my amazement, I found out after years of study and searching that there is no clear agreement on this extremely important issue. For example, Dr Carl Rogers, a highly respected and influential psychologist, believes that a human being is inherently good and free. Given a nurturing environment, Rogers says, a human can be expected to grow and flourish. On the other side of the coin is Sigmund Freud, who considers humans essentially libidinous and fundamentally primitive. Another noted authority Dr B F Skinner, holds that humans are unfree and only imagine that they possess free will.

Who is right? No one has all the evidence unequivocally on their side. In fact, there are probably as many versions about human nature as there are commentators. The most reasonable explanation I've come across regarding our nature comes from social scientists who conclude that we are defined more by the socio-political system in which we happen to reside than by any other factor.

Define yourself

Are you willing to allow yourself to be defined by a political system? In a totalitarian dictatorship, you are not to be trusted. In a political system such as ours, you are worthy of trust. Fortunately, you live in a democratic society and do not have to rely upon the state to tell you who you are. You can decide, if you choose to do so, all on your own.

Who we are is too important an issue to be left to others. In fact, it can only be answered with absolute authority by you and no one else. Of course, there is no shortage of others who will define you if you do not do so yourself. Often these others include well-meaning family members, relatives, friends and people at work. If you are like most people, you will concede that most of your present identity is not really of your own choosing but rather that it has been unwittingly bestowed upon you by society and others. If your present version of your inner self, your real self, is entirely satisfying, then redefining your inner self entirely on your own terms will probably be of little value. However, if you are not getting all that you think is possible out of your life, then redefining your inner self in an effective fashion will undoubtedly enhance the quality of your personal existence.

Most of us have not taken time out in our lives to clarify what this inner self is really like. Some people's inner selves are very negative and very demanding. 'You're no good. You don't deserve better.' Others have an inner self that is freeing, liberating. 'You're a decent person, you deserve a good life. As important as it is, often the definition has been left to develop in slipshod fashion, and therefore it becomes necessary that you take it upon yourself (rather than leave it to less-qualified others) to define (or redefine) your inner self in such a way that it is your friend, your ally, your supporter. This is of prime significance, because it is true that 'as you see yourself, you shall become.'

If you see yourself as flawed, inept, losing, you can be sure that is what you will be. If you see yourself (at the inner-core level) as possessing inner calm, having excitement and adventure as well as purpose and meaning in your life – then undoubtedly that is the kind of life you will have in store for you.

Inner vs outer self

As noted earlier, each of us has two identities, a public or external identity and a private, internal identity. Your external identity is a product of the various 'roles' that you play every day: mother or father, worker, executive, Tory, Labour, Liberal. Your external identity is important, especially, for managing (or surviving) in the day-to-day world, for raising children, earning a living, and so forth. But your inner identity is even more important. This is the place where you really live. The self that you talk to when you are alone or faced with a problem and the conversations you have with this, your inner self, are undoubtedly the most important conversations you can possibly have. If you miss-hit the tennis ball, do you say to yourself, 'Damn you. Can't you keep your eye on the ball?'

Or, do you say, 'Well, nice try. Just do better next time.' Each of us treats ourself differently in similar circumstances.

Who is this self that you speak to, in your mind's eye? It is the *inner* you.

Your inner self is always with you, of course. It is this inner self that you consult and address when you are alone, about to make a decision, when you are worried, creating, or doing. Sometimes this inner self of yours acts as an ally, a friend and sometimes not. Sometimes we treat it roughly. ('Damn you. Why did you do that? You know better.') Less often, we treat it kindly. ('You know, you're really a nice person. I'm proud of you.')

You, obviously, are only one person, but that person is defined primarily by the quality and character of ones inner self. There are three basic types of personalities:

1 inner-managed (the most effective type),

2 outer-dominated (a very high percentage of the population), or

3 outer-controlled (the most defective type).

Effective thinkers (type 1) have a very strong, healthy, free, inner self as I have shown in the diagram that follows. The white space is the outer self, and the darkened area represents the inner self. Notice that generous portions of the healthy inner self spill over to the surface.

Being *dominated* by the externals of life (job, money, image, material possessions, etc) is not as negative as being controlled by externals. The outer-dominated person is as follows:

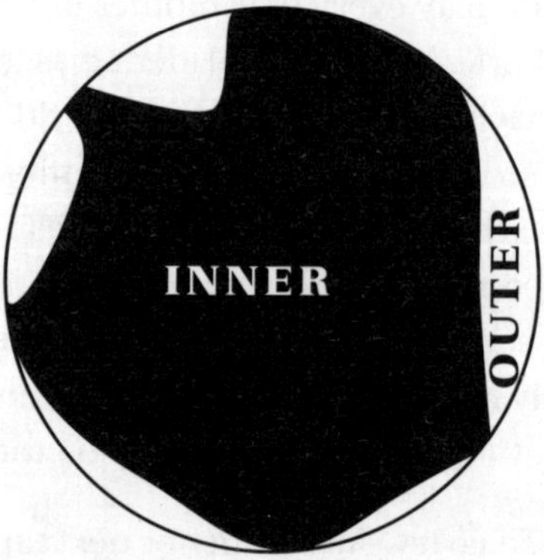

Observe that the externals, while substantial, do not obliterate the inner self.

The wall on the outside is much thicker. The core of inner self is smaller and almost totally confined, but with some outlets. The outer-dominated person, describes a very high percentage of the world's population. The outer-dominated person has a flawed vision of his/her inner self. He/she feels a bit trapped, a bit confused and says, 'But that's the way it is.' Of course, effective thinkers disagree, vehemently.

The outer-*controlled* person is really a victim of anything external he/she happens to encounter. Totally defined by externals, having little or no recognition of the fact that the potential for a strong inner self even exists, he/she has no capacity for introspecting: name, job title, social roles are everything. Seen graphically, he/she looks like this (*opposite*):

Much of your present identity has been derived from 'roles' and years of conditioning. Your present general identity has been derived largely from your contacts with, presumably, well-meaning parents, teachers and friends. Even your children, if you have any, have probably taken a crack at defining you as well. 'Mummy/Daddy,' a son/daughter says with annoyance, 'do you want to know what I think of you as a parent?' 'Sure, darling, please tell me who I am,' they might respond, listening with guilt. Most of your present identity, however, was probably determined before the age of five. It is in those early years that we are most impressionable. Your definition of your inner self, if it has been defined at all, was more than likely not really of your own choosing. Even something as personal as your given name is not of your own choosing. My ears literally perk up when I hear my name, just like Pavlov's dog. Nothing more than a conditioned response! All of us are products of heavy conditioning. Even much of the clothing that we ostensibly choose to wear, our little mannerisms and perhaps even the way that we walk and talk, are the result of long-term conditioning. There are all kinds of models and reinforcers bearing down on us. We've been managed and processed, call it socialisation, ever since birth, facing innumerable authority figures, massive advertising and sloganeering, and all kinds of influential suggestions that badger us day after day on TV and in print. It is no wonder that the question 'Who are you?' tends to intimidate when we ask this of our inner selves.

A 35 year old sales manager with three children and an insensitive husband came to me for counselling in a very confused state of mind. 'About four years ago, I had a complete nervous breakdown,' she said, 'and I turned myself in at the local mental hospital. I was there for a period of two weeks, and eventually, with the help of psychotherapy, my depression lifted somewhat, and I was released of my own accord. Since then, I've been barely managing to get by, day by day and since my breakdown, I've *discarded all the roles* I had been given, but I still don't know who I am. Sure, I was given a very rigid upbringing and I was very religious. I wasn't even permitted to think 'improper' thoughts. Well, after my breakdown, I discarded all that. I no longer wanted to be the perfect mother, the perfect wife – the perfect anything.

'But now that I've discarded all that, I'm still left with the question 'Who am I?' 'I frankly don't know.' This woman did not find her external identities (sales manager and wife) effective. Sadly, until I helped her to access her hidden identity, she had no backup identity to serve her in good stead.

Who are you really?

In a sense, the question 'Who are you?' is almost unfair to ask. Yet it is precisely this question that you must answer. You have an inner-self and you can define it entirely on your own terms. Have you ever really tried to define yourself your way? Your inner self is certainly not your job title, so you cannot comfortably hide behind that. Job titles are external, not inner descriptions of self. Nor is your inner self the other social roles that you might play. Your inner self is much deeper than these conventional social roles.

You may be saying, 'Wait, I know who I am. I'm me.' But just who is that vague, extremely ambiguous, quite amorphous 'me' to whom you refer?

It is essential that you at long last define your inner self in a unique, original, and satisfying manner. Only then can you set in motion a productive prophecy for yourself that will lead to your own inner liberation. During a recent seminar which I conducted, each member of the group suggested identities for the inner selves of the others. Finally, it was left for each member to choose his/her own inner identity. Song and book titles, countries, even names of famous paintings, have been effectively used to describe this part of self. The names selected are only a symbol of one's private version of self. Certainly job titles, social roles, even our given names, tend to place us into 'little boxes' that sometimes seriously limit our potential. So in order to escape from such boxes you must take on a new version of you.

The client, cited earlier, who lost track of who she was after she dropped her conventional roles, created a very exciting secret inner identity for herself during the course of my counselling with her. This new inner identity of hers, which she herself created, proved infinitely more serviceable than the social roles that others had foisted on her – and which resulted in her nervous breakdown.

She described her secret new identity as follows: 'I see a beautiful white bird, a dove, flying with an olive branch in one of its claws. I can remember early in my life admiring such a bird. This dove is circling gracefully round and round above a sturdy boat, a boat that is moving purposefully along in a calm, blue sea. The boat seems to be heading somewhere, somewhere significant, somewhere worthwhile. Somehow I sense this boat will be able to make it safely through all kinds of weather, waters calm and waters rough. I find this a very soothing picture. And this whole picture is me.'

For this woman, this secret inner identity acted as the centre point around which she was able to balance the many confusing facets of her real-life situation as mother, wife, school official officer, and person. When things become complex or upsetting for her, as they sometimes do, she shuts her eyes and returns to her inner vision of herself – for solace, for support, for direction.

I, too, have a picture of my inner self that has served me countless times in very good stead.

For example, one time I was required to wait in a long line at the passport office. The line seemed endless, and my own paranoia made me believe that the clerks were deliberately spiting me because I was in a hurry. Then, suddenly, I realised that I was getting my insides in a tumult. 'What kind of way is this for a Gentle-Flowing Brook (my definition of my inner self) to operate?' I thought, 'I'm acting more like a damned roaring ocean.' Then I got in touch with what I was thinking and feeling and made it a point to take charge.

I closed my eyes for a moment and clearly visualised in my mind's eye a beautiful, crystal-clear, gently flowing brook, a brook that I remember experiencing one summer in the Swiss Alps. My whole body slowed down. Gentle, flowing. Ease. Calm. Moving gently – someplace – who knows where, to a larger body of clear water perhaps and as you can imagine, my whole system slowed down. Gone was the roaring ocean and there I stood ever so calmly and comfortably in line – waiting my turn. Enjoying sight, sound, feeling, being alive and all at no charge. Definitely a personal ecological event. Treating yourself decently is no reason to feel guilty, it is a social contribution and all at no charge – a quiet, qualitative, inner-liberating experience. You don't have to try to improve the whole world to improve the lot of mankind.

Once equipped with a very clear image of your inner self, never again will you be caught fumbling when asking yourself 'Who am I really?' You will be able to answer in terms of your inner-self definition, not in terms of those social role games that most persons are limited to. Remember, if you don't define yourself this way, there are plenty of other persons, well-meaning and not so well-meaning, who will be more than glad to do so, as they have been doing for years.

In my own mind, with my own private name for my inner self – Gentle Flowing Brook – I imagine a very special, particularly beautiful brook, flowing along, lightly, easily, sometimes through rough areas, yet always moving along. The brook is flowing somewhere that is very worthwhile, eventually uniting with a large body of water a crystal clear, blue glacier lake. This image that I have found offers me hope, providing as it does for my uniting with something larger than myself. The gentle flowing of the brook symbolises for me the inner calm that I so cherish. Also, its spontaneous turns through forests and its small waterfalls for me symbolise adventure. When needed, I can draw great nourishment from this special vision of inner self which I alone created. I find this self-picture comforting, reassuring, and revitalising, and I take pride in the fact that this version of myself is one that is totally of my own design and choosing. No one else in the entire world can define myself better than I can. And I have.

Your inner metaphor

In order to create a clear inner-self picture, permit your imagination free rein. Use metaphors if you like, metaphors from nature, art, literature, everyday life. Even images of cars or TV products are fair game. You are restricted only by the limits of your imagination. It is important, before you tackle this self-imaging task, that you fully appreciate its significance. Remember, for example, that the picture you see need not symbolise you as you are but rather as you would like to become. Later you will see why elements of inner calm, purpose, and adventure are important parts of this image, but try to include them now – even if the reason is not yet absolutely clear to you.

The picture that you are about to imagine should have some elements of peace and quiet connected with it – signifying the inner calm that the self managing person finds so necessary. In addition, try to have your picture reflect a sense of hope, of going somewhere – a sense of purpose. Also, include movement in your vision – to symbolise adventure, the third element of inner liberation.

Find a comfortable position; then shut your eyes and permit your imagination free play for five minutes and see what you can come up with. Don't worry about doing it 'right' because if you don't like what you see just now, you can try any time you like later on – and then use the best of your various imaginative creations.

Once you are able to successfully create a vital picture of your inner self, you have established the basis for your own self-fulfilling prophecy. Whenever you find that you are confused or anxious or in a 'box' not of your own choosing, you can turn to this self-picture for support, clarification and nourishment. Without such a picture, you are easy prey for the capricious whims of society and the very limiting social definitions upon which you are tempted to predicate your life. Isn't it far better to have a concept of your inner self that is completely of your own creation rather than having to rely on what others, caring or not, have foisted upon you? As you return to this inner picture of self, time and time again, it becomes the real 'you.' But wait. How about a name for this new version of you, a handle, so that you can remind yourself more conveniently who you really are whenever you need to do so?

Choose your own 'handle'

Overleaf are some **adjectives** and **nouns** which can be used in various combinations to give your self managing inner self an appropriate name. The list is made up of suggestions only. You might have your own ideas for such a name.

Metaphor adjectives

Mellow	Loving	Balanced
Flowing	Warm	Adventurous
Gentle	High	Rambling
Centring	Free	Open
Feeling	Clear	Caring
Healthy	True	Calming
Lively	Flexible	Easy
New	Calm	Rolling

Metaphor nouns

Stream	Song	Heart
Eagle	Boat	Spirit
Seagull	Cloud	Brook
Bike	Forest	Ocean
Rose	Rolls Royce	Mountain
Seeker	Leaf	Flower
Dancer	Opera	Apple
Flower bed	Castle	Dawn

Try out various combinations to see how they sound. A new name by itself serves little purpose; it needs an image that goes along with it. Perhaps the name you select can supplement the image you already focused upon, or better still, help this inner-self picture of yours still more. Make up a few names and try them on for size. Again, you're not limited to this list but come up, at least tentatively, with a 'handle' for your inner self. Take a few minutes and do this now. Have some fun in the process. Experiment. If you don't find what you've done completely satisfying, try again. I cannot emphasise enough how important it is that you have a very clear and imaginative picture of your inner self, how useful a name for this picture is in helping you remind yourself who you really are when circumstances warrant such a reminder. It is so easy to be pulled off centre by your job, by many of life's circumstances, even by your family. But if you know who you are at the inner self level, you will become immune to the traps, boxes, and conditions that often confuse most others. 'After all,' you will think to yourself, 'why does a Lively Spirit have to become upset over that?'

Another one of my clients, Cedric, a 58 year old tax accountant who had suffered a heart attack a year before coming to me for counselling applied this method. Cedric defined his inner self as a flower bed. He said that he chose a flower bed because he always loved gardening, although he had little time to work at this love of his. 'As a flower bed, I see things grow, and then when they die, they soften the bed, add to it, make it more fertile and possible for new plants to spring forth. I find, being a flower bed, that I am now more resilient and hopeful than I ever was before. Unfortunately, my heart attack was brought on because I took the pressures of my tax work too seriously. Also I always felt that my family put lots of pressure on me as a father and as a husband. It was too much. Now during my busiest time at the office, when some of my particularly demanding clients are at their worst, I think to myself, 'What has getting upset over taxes and deadlines got to do with being a flower bed?' I'm more relaxed now than I've ever been in my entire life. I only wish I knew that I was a flower bed before I got my attack.' Chances are, if he had, such an attack might have been avoided.

Even if you haven't made a final decision as to your new name, make a tentative one. Write it down in the margin of this book. Then check it out later and see if you still like it. If it doesn't quite suit you, then, change it. Find one that does. It can really alter your life, even prolong it.

Accessing your hidden identity

The following exercise will help you to access your own inner identity. Everyone has one. The renowned Swiss psychiatrist, Carl Gustav Jung, theorised that in the minds of all of us are certain universal symbols that are passed down from generation to generation (the collective unconscious). The trick is to draw upon these universals by bringing them up from the sub or unconscious to the conscious, as and when needed.

Instructions. Read the following script into a tape recorder and then play it back to yourself periodically. Find a quiet and comfortable place where you can concentrate without interruption for about five or six minutes. That's all that it will take for you to listen to the tape. The script opposite, will suggest that (in your mind's eye) you visit a place of great beauty where you first experience a sense of great inner calm, then experience a sense of purposefulness and finally a sense of adventure. Then all three of these ingredients are to be experienced in concert. At that point you will be asked to name this experience as if you were naming a vacation retreat, a summer home, or a boat. You will engrave this memory into your conscious mind and slowly open your eyes. The name and picture that you, and you alone, originated will become, if you want it to be, your back-up hidden identity. It will, as promised, have incorporated within it the life enriching qualities of calm, purpose and adventure and it will serve you as a useful short-cut to greater life satisfaction.

SCRIPT (TO PUT ON TAPE RECORDER) TO ACCESS YOUR HIDDEN IDENTITY

Please shut your eyes. Now listen carefully and follow the instructions that I give you. Shut your eyes even tighter. Tighter still. Now let the little muscles on your eyelids relax. Now make your forehead very tense and very tight. Now relax your forehead. Let all the muscles in your forehead relax. Now become aware of the back of your neck. Be aware of all of the tension that may have accumulated there, in the back of your neck. Now let the back of your neck relax, completely. Now be aware of your upper and lower jaws. Be aware of any tension there and now let your upper and lower jaws separate ever so slightly. Let your jaws relax. Now do the same for your right arm and shoulder. Be very much aware of tension in your right arm and shoulder and now let your shoulder and right arm relax completely. That's fine. That's very, very good. Now your left arm and shoulder. Make your left arm and shoulder very tight and very tense. Now let your left arm and shoulder relax. Now as you breath in, imagine that you are breathing in airs of relaxation and then as you breath out, that you are breathing all tension in your system out. Breathing in, very slowly, airs of relaxation. As you breath out, airs of tension out. *(Pause.)* Good. Now in your mind's eye, visit your spinal column. As you know, your spinal column is connected to your entire nervous system. Now make your spinal column tense and tight for a moment. That's right, tension in your spinal column. Now let your entire spinal column relax. Let your entire spinal column relax. Very good. And now your whole nervous system is relaxing. Breathing in very slowly airs of relaxation and exhaling any remaining tension that you might still have. *(Pause.)* Now be aware of your right leg. Make it tense and tight. Good. Now let your right leg relax completely. Let it get tired and limp. And now your left leg. Be aware of your left leg. Make it tense and tight. And now let your left leg relax completely. Now you are very, very relaxed. *(Pause.)*

Now imagine that you are in a very comfortable lift, and you are sitting in a very comfortable chair in that lift. You can decide now whether you want the lift to go up, or if you want the lift to go down. Decide now, if you prefer to go up or down in the lift. *(Pause.)* Fine, the lift is going to go in that direction. Now I am going to count backwards from 10 to 1 and with each number the lift is going to take you progressively closer to a place of great beauty. A place of fantastic, exquisite beauty. Ready now. **Ten**. The lift is moving you along and you are feeling better than you have done in a very long time. **Nine**. Moving along very comfortably, very relaxed. *(Pause.)* **Eight**. Moving along to a place of great beauty. **Seven**. You are doing very well. *(Pause.)* You are moving closer and closer to your destination, a place of utterly fantastic, great beauty. **Six**. The lift is continuing to move you along and you are feeling very, very comfortable and relaxed. Moving along toward a place of great beauty. **Five**. Moving along more and more. Very relaxed. Very comfortable. The lift is taking you to a wonderful place of great beauty. **Four**. Very comfortable. Very, very relaxed. You haven't been this comfortable, this much at ease in a very long time. **Three**. Moving along very comfortably, very relaxed. *(Pause.)* **Two**. Moving along now and getting very, very close to your destination. Very close to your place of great beauty. You are doing very well. *(Pause.)* You are moving closer and closer to your destination, a place of utterly fantastic, great beauty. And now, at last, **one**. You have arrived at your destination and the lift door opens and there it is – a place of absolutely fantastic, gorgeous, marvellous beauty. You move effortlessly out of the lift into this marvellous, beautiful tranquil place. Now take it all in. Smell it. Taste it. Feel it. Experience it in your own way with all of your senses for the next 20 seconds. *(Pause for about 20 seconds.)* Now you are experiencing a great sense of inner peace. Of inner tranquillity. Of inner calm. Experience your sense of inner calm in your own way for the next 20 seconds or so. *(Pause for about 20 more seconds.)* Now, off in the distance, you sense something wonderful, something very important and wonderful going on, but you are not all that clear about what it is. All you know is that you are needed there. So now you find yourself moving effortlessly toward this other wonderful place off in the distance. You sense that it is important that you go there. Now pause for an additional 20 seconds or so and visit your sense of purpose. *(Pause for about 20 seconds.)* You have a great sense of importance. A feeling of mission, off in the distance, where you are needed. And now experience the sense of adventure as you calmly, effortlessly are moving forward on your mission. Experience a sense of exhilaration and excitement combined with your inner calm and sense of purpose. Experience your sense of adventure, in your own way over the next 20 seconds. *(Pause again, for about 20 seconds.)*

Now you are experiencing a great sense of inner calm, combined with a great sense of purpose, combined with a great sense of adventure. Experience now the combination of calm, purpose and adventure all at once. Calm, purpose and adventure. Experience yourself this way for the next minute. In your own way. *(Pause now for about 60 seconds.)* You have just experienced yourself at your innermost level. Now give this experience of yours a name, as if you are naming a holiday retreat, a summer home, or a ship. Perhaps an exotic or mysterious name. Whatever name comes to you just now. *(Pause.)* Now repeat that name that you have just come up with to yourself. Now repeat that name to yourself, slowly, three more times. This name is you, at the inner self level. You will remember this name and be able to use it any time that you want to remind yourself to be calmer, more purposeful and more adventurous. OK, now answer these questions. Who are you? Now repeat the name of your hidden identity. Yes, but who are you really? *(Same name.)* Yes, I know what you have said. But who is the real you. *(Same name.)*

You will remember everything that you have done during this exercise. You will remember your hidden identity and be able to use it any time you want to. It can be one of your most valuable effective thoughts. Now in a moment, I am going to ask you to open your eyes and then you will pause and remind yourself of this entire experience. **One**. You are now feeling very refreshed. **Two**. Sit up in your chair now. **Three**. Now open your eyes. You are feeling very refreshed and very calm.

(end of script)

Now turn your tape recorder off and take some time for reflection. Then answer the following in the spaces provided.

My hidden identity name is:

____

For each of us, this exercise will produce something a bit different. If you are not entirely satisfied with the picture or name that rose up from your own subconscious, you can do it again, whenever you choose to do so. It is important, if you are to master yourself, that you access an identity that has calm, purpose and adventure structured within it.

The name 'mellow tourist' for example, brought to one person, calm, purpose and adventure in the following way: 'my inner calm came from my walking about as a tourist, unencumbered with ordinary day-to-day problems. Each turn was a surprise. That was my sense of adventure. And my purpose, I suppose, came from having a general itinerary for my journey. I was going somewhere, even while I stopped to take in the sights.'

Some of the hidden identity names that others who did this same exercise discovered were: Mountain High, Valhalla, Harmony, My Secret Place, Gentle Flowing Brook (mine), Daybreak on the Beach, Easy Passage, Souring Eagle, Open Sky, Gliding Light and many others, mostly derived from nature. Even such less exotic names as Rolling Rolls Royce, Prospering Executive and CEO in Charge of Myself proved extremely helpful to certain people.

In order to further examine your 'experience' with this exercise, please answer the following questions:

What did you experience when you were moving forward effortlessly with a sense of purpose?

____

____

____

How, exactly did you feel when you combined calm, purpose and adventure?

____

____

____

This exercise will work for you, only if you concentrate on it and only if you want it to work. Repeat doing it until it begins to take root for you. Those who take this exercise seriously report that it definitely adds to their inner life.

Who knows better than you about who you really are? Why don't you employ your new found inner identity that you alone have just created for yourself? You see, once we get into the *effective thinking* process itself, you'll see how your 'hidden identity' can serve as an effective thought whenever you want to attain greater levels of calm, purpose or adventure.

It is important that you never forget who you are. So that you can reinforce this, ask yourself the two following questions periodically: *'What is it that I want out of my life?'* (Remember to separate your desires from your needs); (2nd) *'Who am I?'* (Shut your eyes, return to that inner picture of you, and experience it with your whole being). Then mention your secret name to yourself to remind yourself who you really are, regardless of what others might call you.

With your hidden identity readily available to you, you no longer need to take criticism personally. After all, it will only be your external image that is being criticised and not your true inner self. Who would seriously criticise anyone if all they wanted was a full and satisfying life, but not at the expense of any other person? Who would want to criticise anyone who was calm, had a sense of purpose and plenty of adventure in their life, at the inner self level?

ELEVEN

Managing your emotions

Effective thinkers, when necessary, can take full charge of their emotional life. Your emotions, your feelings take place under your own skin. You are the world's leading authority on how you feel at all times and in all places. Effective thinkers, consequently, make it their business to take full charge of their own emotional life, whenever it makes sense to do so. Why not?

To what degree, under what circumstances and toward what ends, do you permit your emotions free rein? How do you moderate your emotional expression so that it serves you best? What are the effective thoughts that produce a more satisfying emotional life for you?

Emotions are feelings – visceral experiences, internal *responses*, that result from the thoughts you choose. If you take away the thought, you also take away the *feeling* that the thought produces. An infant is born with a simple sense of pleasure and pain. There is little that is as pure as an infant's total expression of glee and joy. Nor is there anything more intense than that infant's scowl and cry of displeasure. Gradually, as the infant's capacity to think is refined, his emotional responses become proportionately more complex until he has acquired a full range of emotional expressions. These are all *learned* by choosing thoughts. The child learns fear, joy, worry, anger, love, confidence, hate, and many more emotions, some producing inner satisfaction, others disrupting the quality of his inner life. He learns that loud sounds are not necessarily always to be feared. Take a small child to his/her first football game at a crowded football ground on a Saturday afternoon. As the teams come onto the pitch, the crowd lets out a mighty roar. The long-awaited game is about to get underway, but look at the child.

He/she is crouched in stark fear, the roar of the crowd (most naturally) is frightening him/her half to death. So he/she looks despondently to you for guidance.

'It's all right,' you say. 'It's all right. No need to be frightened,' you say as you pull him/her close to you. 'This is just a game and the crowd always roars when it starts.' So he/she learns from you that there is sometimes pleasure in 'roaring,' and he/she adds still another lesson to his/her emotional vocabulary.

Emotional vocabulary

Anger ■ Happiness ■ Anxiety ■ Hate ■ Calm ■ Innocence Confidence ■ Jealousy ■ Depression ■ Joy ■ Despair ■ Liking Disgust ■ Love ■ Ecstasy ■ Mellowness ■ Fear ■ Sadness Generosity ■ Tension ■ Guilt ■ Worry

There are many feelings that escape accurate description. Words at best approximate feelings. Yet it is with words that we create the thoughts that bring these feelings to life. The key that controls your feelings is firmly within your grasp. You know how to choose effective thoughts, thoughts that lead to a more satisfying emotional existence. 'More satisfying' includes the full range of human emotion, so your key permits you to let yourself go emotionally, to be stupid and foolish, even to be excessively emotional should circumstances warrant such feelings. Occasional emotional excesses can serve as useful stimulants. However, 'paralysing fear,' 'ulcer-producing anger,' 'bile-producing jealousy,' or 'heart-attack-producing worry' are defective. It is through your choosing more effective thoughts that such emotions can be readily brought under control.

Control is not repression

To regularly repress an emotion can lead to psychosomatic illness. A person who walks around with a smile on his face while he is burning up with repressed fury risks psychosomatic heart disease, peptic ulcers, migraine headaches, backaches, and even more severe diseases. Self-managing control of your emotions is quite different from repression. If you hardly ever get angry, it may look to others as though you are holding back your true feelings, but if these others knew how you really were looking at life, they would see that you are not repressing angry feelings – that in fact you are not experiencing these feelings at all. You, for example, might call me a rude name, but if I did not presume that you were really referring to me, you would hardly expect me to be angry. This, in essence, is how self -managing people insulate themselves from feeling anything at all that is unwanted or useless.

Fear

Whenever the self managing person experiences one of the less than satisfying emotions – anger, worry, guilt, jealousy, etc – he/she quickly asks himself, 'What am I *afraid of*?' After identifying the fear and removing the basis for that fear, he/she finds that the secondary emotion, anger, jealousy, etc simply dissolves. It is not repressed or held back, it simply vanishes. The fear upon which it has been based has been removed. Of course, if an effective line of thought cannot be found to overcome the fear, then the secondary emotion will continue to gain momentum and another tactic will be needed. However, since effective thinkers have so many thoughts in their repertoire to help them overcome most fears, it is not usually necessary for them to go beyond this first stage.

Once you have perfected your 'I can handle it' attitude and have acquired all the traits that go with calm, purpose and adventure, you will rarely feel intimidated, put upon, or threatened. When you have worked through and accepted the various inner-liberating facts (such as 'life can sometimes be very unfair,' or 'part of you is truly alone'), you will rarely be caught short and in turn frightened. Of course, the few times that you are caught short, you must immediately begin a working through process to accept certain facts, so that you can overcome the fear you are experiencing.

When you get angry, as you inevitably will from time to time (being caught short), you must not deny or repress this feeling but instead, quickly and energetically change your mindset and examine the basis of the fear that has produced this unwanted emotion.

There are in this world, obviously, some conditions genuinely worth fearing: pain, actual danger to yourself, actual danger to your loved ones, etc. The animal response to fear – characterised by an increase of adrenaline in your system, a tight stomach, a clenched jaw and fist and shortness of breath – is a natural response, the 'flight or fight' response, so necessary in nature. With the increase of adrenaline, we are able to muster a surprising amount of energy to deal with actual emergencies.

Men have been known to leap over seven foot walls when frightened sufficiently, whereas normally they could just about make it up a stairway. Women have been known to fight off assailants literally twice their size when sufficiently incited by fear.

Fear can be an extremely useful and valuable emotional response, but unnecessary fear can do us tremendous harm.

Those who operate in a *fearful* emotional state unnecessarily and too often, produce flight or fight physiological stresses – adrenaline, the tensing of the stomach, etc but in a repressed form. Consequently, they harm both their bodies and their emotional systems. In addition, they often lash out and harm those around them.

Overcoming unwanted anger

Fear is the basis of anger. If a fear is warranted, the anger that results is warranted too. If a bear emerges from the woods and frightens you, you run. You end up angry that the bear intruded in your path and sent you sailing. Quite reasonable. If your friend doesn't meet you at the appointed hour and you wait and wait, your fear that you will be left, or that you don't count to your friend as much as you thought, leads to frustration and anger. Is your anger warranted in this situation in view of what you have learned about effective thinking? Of course not.

If you did not have the unwarranted fear, then no anger would have resulted. The way to counter anger in this case is to simply remove the unwarranted fear. Choose thoughts such as this: 'I don't know how important I am to this friend of mine. I know that I may be of some importance, but my friend has his/her own hierarchy of relationships and needs. In any case, I am still a loveable person. So why be fearful and then angry? I'll just make it my business to enjoy myself while I am waiting. Perhaps I'll sit down and read a magazine, or prepare my next talk to the company and wait to see if my friend turns up. If not, I'll go on to lunch by myself and enjoy my senses. Such is life.'

Fear is merely a state of mind. In the same way that unwarranted fear can lead to unnecessary anger, it can also lead to other unwanted, usually useless, emotions: worry, guilt and jealousy.

Feigned anger can be useful

If you decide that the anger you are experiencing is useless (as it generally is), you can easily feign anger rather than really experience it, thus saving your adrenaline, your stomach, and your heart.

One of my clients, Joyce, a 27 year old nurse, was experiencing debilitating anger toward her son. However, she learned to control her young son, Jason, by feigning anger, giving him a stern look. Sometimes she clenched her fist and even stomped her foot, but inside, Joyce learned not to be angry at all. She simply came to realise that her son responded to the impression that 'Mummy is really angry.' Her imitation of being angry got him moving much more quickly than her former uncontrolled anger did. By pretending anger, Joyce produced exactly the same effect as she would have done if she had actually torn up her insides with real anger. Since Joyce had developed a batch of effective thoughts to prevent being manipulated by others, and since she was secure regardless of how Jason behaved, she had overcome the basis for genuine anger toward Jason.

Overcoming worry

Worry is a word you could readily eliminate from your vocabulary if you didn't need it to describe what so many *others* do. Self-managing people make it their business not to worry about anything. They do, however, replace worry with *due concern* when appropriate. Certainly it is wise to make plans for future contingencies. This is *due concern*. 'Due concern' implies creative anxiety and a plan of action, whereas 'worry' suggests the useless spinning of your wheels – busily going nowhere.

It is possible to worry about everything that has fear as its basis. You can worry about retirement, your job, your relationships, your health, your loved ones, the political situation, money, your life, your death – or even fear itself, but worry accomplishes absolutely nothing.

Worry is based upon the fear that something unpleasant or negative is going to happen in the future. Then, through our imagination, we visceral experience this negative event. We think of our loved ones out in a car on the highway. We hear the screeching brakes, the crash; we see their bruised and bleeding bodies. We shudder. Our palms sweat. Our adrenaline pumps. We anguish, physically as well as mentally. It is real as far as our bodies are concerned and the toll on our hearts, our stomachs, our lives, is real.

Most of what we worry about never takes place.

Recently I flew to California to give a lecture. When I arrived, the airline reported that my baggage was lost. 'We think it might have gone on to Hong Kong,' the clerk said apologetically. I decided in advance that I was not going to worry, even though a portion of a book manuscript (quite irreplaceable) was in my suitcase. Here was my line of reasoning:

'First of all, I will not worry because it will not change anything. If the bag and the manuscript are lost, I'll take care of that step by step. All I really have in this life is my mind and body anyhow. As far as the clothing in the bag – well, that is all replaceable. It will cost some money, but I can take care of that. As far as the manuscript – well, that will hurt. So – ouch. If it is gone, I'll just start on another. Who said life is fair?

'After all, here I am in a wonderful place and since I have a permanent sabbatical attitude, I'm going to enjoy myself, even if I wear these same clothes every day that I'm here, or even if I have to go out and buy some. Then again, it is also possible that my baggage will show up and if it does, I'll be in good shape.'

Needless to say, the next day the bags were found and sent to my hotel with apologies. Honestly, I lost no sleep, had not one bit of anguish (other than momentarily, until I reminded myself of the proper mindset and chose the necessary effective thoughts). Worry is just not part of my inner-liberating bargain with myself.

One of my clients shared a similar attitude which he had developed concerning his 20 year old daughter, who was driving around late at night. 'Then I figured out that as much as I didn't like it, there wasn't anything that I could do about it. She's old enough now to take responsibility for herself. God forbid, if she was in an accident. All I could do would be to ensure she got the best treatment, go and see her, show her that I care and try to help. Worrying wasn't helping at all, so I decided to stop it and I did.'

We usually don't worry about something at the moment it is happening because when it is actually happening, we must deal with it instantly. You're not in the *process* of worrying while the boss is telling you off – you are too busy taking care of the situation then and there. If you stick yourself with a pin, you aren't worrying that you will be stuck with a pin – you are too actively engaged in saying 'Ouch' and moving the pin away so that you won't be stuck again. When dealing with the 'here and now,' there is no time to worry. Think to yourself: 'What if the worst happens?' See yourself dealing effectively with it, and then forget about it.

The next time you find yourself thinking ahead about some dreadful thing that might happen, take your imagination one important step further. Imagine that the worst has actually happened and figure out how you will survive.

The following approach may sound a bit cavalier, but for some people it works. If this is an issue of yours, give it a try. It may just work for you.

Imagine that the plane you were planning to take crashes. See yourself as badly injured. You crawl around for help. You are so very busy surviving or trying to survive that you have no time for worry. You will be able to ask yourself the three calming questions: What time is it? 'Now.' Where am I? 'Here.' Who is that person I am with? 'Me.' No matter what your situation, providing your mind still works, you will still be able to choose effective thoughts. You know that you will handle it – even should the worst take place – once you have become an effective thinker.

Next think of this: the dangers of an air crash are less than if you were to drive your car. Due concern, not worry, will prove helpful. If you take an airline with a good safety record, you improve the odds in your favour.

Listen to the flight steward as you are given instructions on exits and emergency procedures. Due concern again. Go and enjoy yourself. Certainly if worry were to help, it would be worthwhile for you to choose worrisome thoughts. Since worry offers absolutely nothing except ulcerating prospects, face the facts of life, treat the worrisome thoughts with due concern – and forget to worry ever again.

Overcoming useless guilt

If worry is based upon fear of what's ahead, then guilt is fear about what has already happened. And if worry is useless, then guilt – genuine, unrelenting guilt – is even more useless.

It makes sense to make amends for something you are sorry you did and it is intelligent to make plans not to repeat your errors. But again, it makes no sense to worry – especially about what has already happened.

If yesterday or sometime in the past you said or did something that was unkind to someone, it serves no purpose whatsoever for you to feel guilty. You cannot undo that which you have already done. You had better spend your time doing something positive for that person now, if still possible, rather than lament what you should have done.

Some will argue that if you have committed a crime you ought to feel guilty and punish yourself, but it does no good to 'get even' with yourself. If a government finds you guilty for a wrongdoing and penalises you with prison or a fine, that makes some sense, if such punishment acts as a deterrent for subsequent wrongdoing, but it makes no sense whatsoever for you to penalise yourself. For example, if you are found guilty for speeding, you can accept society's punishment, especially if the punishment suits the offence, but there is no need to punish yourself twice. Your response to any 'wrong' act that you've done, should be present and future oriented, not past oriented. 'What can I do now or in the future that can help me avoid doing such wrong again?' is a sensible question. But self-punishment (prolonged guilt) does nothing for anyone, least of all you.

Once I unfairly scolded my daughter when she was about five years old. I apologised, 'Lynne, I'm sorry.' My daughter, much wiser than I, retorted, 'Sorry's not enough.' And she was right.

Once a present moment passes, it will never be yours to spend again. At least not in reality. You might dream or fantasise about what you might have done or what might have been, but in reality there is no going back and trying to replay it. Life is not a film, where you can reshoot it. Therefore, to worry about what has already happened (feeling guilty) is perfectly useless. It keeps you from using your present moments much more effectively. 'Sorry isn't enough!'

We all make mistakes, do foolish and even stupid things. After all, we are only human. Since it makes no sense to berate ourselves, what should we do?

Take a tennis game as an example. Your doubles partner makes a strong shot. Your opponent returns softly. You move in for the kill, but for a moment, you take your eye off the ball, and you miss what should have been an easy point for your side. 'Sorry,' you say to your partner. He gives you a disappointed look. 'Oh my', you say to yourself, 'I'm a fool. I should have kept my eye on the ball. I really let him down. I know that I can do better, too. Oh, do I feel rotten. I am useless.'

Examine what you are doing. 'I am useless.' This is a self-fulfilling prophecy. Is this self-deprecation doing either you or your partner any genuine good? Of course not.

New game point. Opponents are serving. You miss it again. (Why not? You've already called yourself useless.)

How might you have better handled your mistake on the tennis court? Let's have a re-take.

The ball is returned softly to you after your tennis partner hits a resounding smash to your opponents' court. You miss-hit. This time your inner-liberating line of reasoning leaves you guilt-free and with a self-fulfilling prophecy that is much more positive and just as realistic.

'Oh, I miss-hit. Damn it. I goofed. Okay, that's over. Let me visualise that stroke again and imagine that I hit it properly, without taking my eye off the ball. Okay, memory, store that more effective picture for next time.' You are ready now to get on with the next play. 'You're a good player, still.'

Overcoming useless jealousy

Jealousy can be one of the most insidious and debilitating of all emotions. As with worry and guilt, the underlying emotion at the root of jealousy is also unnecessary fear.

Eliminate the basic fear and the jealous feelings will dissolve.

When you think that someone is getting more than you, having it better than you, taking something away from you, you can become jealous. You may not feel jealous if your neighbours drives a new Jaguar, if you happen to drive a new Rolls, but you might get jealous if suddenly those same neighbours are able to afford a Bentley. 'Where does the money come from? They must be doing all right.' You fear that you won't be able to do 'all right' too. You might try not to feel jealous, but deep down it's often there. 'I'm not jealous. I'm glad for them,' you say to your spouse, but even as you speak these very words, there is a dryness in your mouth betraying the lie in your words.

Years ago, one of my close friends, Charles, 'beat me out' on an important academic post. At first I denied to myself that his good fortune bothered me. 'The best man for that job won, that's all. I'm glad for him,' I said to myself wryly.

What made matters worse was that shortly after he won this job, someone arranged a gathering on his behalf. I was invited. 'Great, Charlie' I said, 'I'm really proud of you,' squelching my honest pangs of jealousy.

Finally, after I could stand it no longer, I walked up to him at his party and called him aside for a few moments. I looked him in the eye and said, 'Before we go on, I've got a confession to make.' He waited. 'Charlie,' I said, 'I just want you to know that although I'm glad for you as a person, I'm also very jealous of you, because I wanted that job.'

My confession cleared the air. I could then deal honestly with him for the first time. Then later I could authentically say, 'I'm genuinely pleased for you,' and mean it.

By acknowledging my jealousy, I was able to begin to deal with it and also face the fears that underlie this wasteful, but normal, emotion. By admitting I was jealous, I was able to develop a line of effective thoughts that put the jealousy to rest. The line of thought went something like this:

'First of all, Charlie is Charlie, and I am me. I'm glad to be me. I've got my life, my style, and they suit me. Sure I'd like the job he's got at this point of my life, but in actuality I'm not doing too badly myself I'm certain that some other people wish they could be doing as well as I am. Wherever you go, no matter how far up or down, there's inevitably someone doing a little better than you and someone doing a little worse. What's more, I'm still loveable. I've learned to have a great life regardless of any situation. So, Charles, I honestly wish you well.'

Most of us experience human pangs of jealousy from time to time. 'Why should they (the football players, the movie stars, Royalty) make all that money for what they do? Look at how hard I work, and I don't get nearly what they do!' 'Why is it that so and so got recognition for that when what I did was just as good, perhaps even better?' 'I could have written better than that myself.'

Jealousy results from the fears that arise when we compare ourselves to others. If we didn't compare ourselves, we wouldn't be fearful and jealous, especially if we didn't compare ourselves to those who seem to be doing better than we are. Yet such comparisons are quite normal. It might help for a moment or two to compare yourself to someone who is worse off than you, but the satisfaction from this approach generally doesn't last long.

A little bit of jealousy can sometimes be useful. It could give you the impetus to get started on that project you've long had in mind ('If they can do it, I can do it too'). On the other hand, jealousy that paralyses, that poisons, that makes you miserable, makes you do things that deep down you'd rather not be doing, can readily be eliminated or at least seriously reduced by taking the proper inner-liberating line of thought. Here are the steps:

- *Acknowledge right off that you are jealous.* When you keep denying, even to yourself that you are envious or jealous of another's good fortune, you keep yourself from dealing with it. If you speak directly to the person you are jealous of and say, 'You know, I'm really jealous of your good fortune,' you can then have a much more honest relationship with that person – if such a relationship happens to be important to you. You could also clearly acknowledge the jealousy to yourself and have the same effect.
- *Ask yourself: what am I afraid of that is making me jealous?* Is it that you are not feeling sufficiently loveable or attractive? Is there a fear that you will never gain sufficient recognition in your own right? Is there a fear that you can't have a good life for yourself? Do you fear life and opportunities are passing you by?

All fears such as these can readily be overcome by self-managing thinking. Lovability and attractiveness are part of inner calm. It's pretty hard to stay jealous of anyone when you remember that you have mastered the techniques of calm, purpose, and adventure.

All your emotions, including guilt, worry, even depression, might be worth experiencing to a certain extent, but as one of my clients said recently about feeling depressed, 'It's an okay place to visit, but I'll be damned if I want to live there.'

Enjoying

Most of this section focused on getting rid of or controlling unwanted emotions. Having done that, you are left with the pleasant ones – at least most of the time. Joyful experiences, ecstasy, fun, are all part of the spontaneity that was discussed earlier. In fact, this entire book and the line of effective thoughts presented here are designed to bring you your fair share of the pleasant emotions – calm, purpose, and adventure – so that you can enjoy being self-reliant.

Sometimes, of course, it becomes necessary to moderate or curb joyous emotions too, and the control process is exactly the same. You simply ask yourself what it is that is making you so confident, then choose those thoughts that will make you feel less confident and smug. Thoughts such as the following will readily bring you down to earth when necessary:

- 'I'm only human.'
- 'I, too, will meet the great leveller in due time.'
- 'I can easily be replaced, in many ways.'
- 'I put on my trousers in the morning one leg at a time, just like everybody else.'

Once you are able to manage your emotions by using effective thinking, you will be very much in charge of yourself. After all, as mentioned at the outset of this chapter, your real life takes place under your skin and when you manage your emotions effectively, you will be setting an excellent example for others as well.

Part One Summary

By employing programmes 1 and 2 you will have unlocked the door to successful self management. You will be an effective thinker.

Programme 1: *'Relentlessly aim for a 'full and satisfying life, but not at the expense of any other person.'*

Programme 2: *'Consistently choose the kind of thoughts that will provide you with the full and satisfying life you seek but not at the expense of any other person.'*

Remember to relentlessly keep your mind on having a very high quality of life every day, but not at the expense of any other person. You owe it to yourself – on this your relatively short vacation from eternity. Whenever you find that you are having trouble staying on track, ask yourself some of the following basic questions:

Ask and remind yourself

- Why am I?
- What am I?
- When am I?
- Where am I?
- Who am I?
- How am I?

The answers that you give to any of these fundamental questions is of great importance. Your answers can serve to remind you of your primary life objective (a wonderful life) and how to go about attaining it.

- **Why are you?**

  An effective answer is – 'to have a full and satisfying life, never at the expense of any other person.'

- **What are you?**

  An effective answer to this question – a 'thought chooser', of course. This serves to remind you that you will always have the power to choose any thought that you want and at any time and at any place.

- **When are you?**

  The effective answer is 'now.' How do you make your nows rich and satisfying? By pausing and choosing effective thoughts, of course.

- **Where are you?**

  Answer: Here.

- **Who are you?**

  Answer: a 'Gentle Flowing Brook?' No, that's my hidden identity! Find and choose your own identity and answer with that. Be sure that inner calm, passionate purpose and plenty of fun and adventure are structured into that inner identity of yours. Remember this hidden identity of yours becomes a self-fulfilling prophecy.

- **How are you?**

  Effective answer: 'OK' (or whatever). Be sure to add, 'but the best is yet to come.' Every time you give yourself this answer it is likely to bring a smile to your face. Is it true? Who knows? But it is surely effective, if feeling good about life (not at others' expense) is something you seek.

Again, how does one make his or her life 'full and satisfying.' Answer – *'By pausing and choosing effective, not defective thoughts, time and time again.'*

Remember to choose effective thoughts whenever it makes sense to do so. Remember, the definition of an '**effective thought**' is any thought, whatsoever, that leads directly or indirectly toward the achievement of a full and satisfying life, *but not at the expense of any other person'*

The preceding ten chapters detailed how to relentlessly aim to have a full and satisfying life, not at the expense of any other person. We took you through a series of challenging exercises to help you to deepen your resolve to have such a life. Then we explored all you needed to know in order to take full responsibility for your own thought choosing. We examined how the human mind works and took notice of the powerful fact that it is one's thoughts that produce both feelings and behaviour. We explored how one can build a private effective thought file and we explored some proven ways for managing one's thought files to optimal advantage. Remember, for example, to pause and P-R-E-P. **P** stands for **prefer**, not need. **R** stands for be **realistic**, not merely reasonable. **E** stands for strive for **excellence**, not perfection. The last **P** stands for have **projects**, not problems.

Then we examined how one goes about consciously choosing the effective thoughts from one's files. We explored the importance of taking time to pause in order to break a self-defeating mindset. We took note that in order to buttress one's proactive thought-choosing (Plan A), some *subconscious* thought choosing assistance (Plan B) can be employed.

We reviewed how to use 90 second rapid self hypnosis to assist you in thought choosing at certain times.

Then we concentrated on how to utilise one of the most powerful of all effective thoughts available to any person – one's inner self picture. We showed you how to define yourself with a practical inner metaphor. We examined how to use it to great advantage to tap in on a sense of inner calm, a clarity of purpose and for having sufficient fun and adventure.

Closing reminders

1. Do not be a psychological pauper. Instead, become a psychological millionaire.
2. Go for satisfaction, not happiness.
3. Make a deep commitment to *relentlessly* pursue a great life, but not at the expense of any other person.
4. Remind yourself, constantly, that it is **you** who chooses your own thoughts.
5. Remember, without a correlative thought, you have no feelings and no meaningful behaviour.
6. Remember that the definition of an effective thought is any thought that produces for you (directly or indirectly) a full and satisfying life, but not at the expense of any other person.
7. Consciously, proactively, choose effective thoughts.
8. Don't forget to pause, find and choose an effective thought whenever you notice that you have a self-defeating mindset.
9. If you need some assistance in consciously choosing an effective thought, then utilise rapid (90-second) self-hypnosis, in order to give yourself some subconscious assistance.
10. Draw on your inner picture from time to time, especially when your external definitions of self (job title, family roles, etc, etc) are in a bit of trouble.
11. Manage your emotions by effective thought choosing.
12. Remember that fear is the basis of anger, and most of what you fear is generally unwarranted.
13. If angry or jealous, ask yourself what is it that are you afraid of? Reduce that fear and the anger or jealously will diminish as well.
14. Be sure to successfully manage yourself before you even think seriously of attempting to manage others.

PART TWO

HOW TO SUCCESSFULLY INTERRELATE WITH OTHERS

Overview

Now it is time for programmes 3 and 4.

TWO ADDITIONAL PROGRAMMES OPEN THE DOOR TO SUCCESSFULLY INTERRELATING WITH OTHERS

Programme 3: Periodically assess your interpersonal strengths and weaknesses.

Programme 4: Systematically improve, bit by bit.

Now, if you have read this far, you have put yourselves through programmes 1 and 2 and can successfully get your mind to work for you. At this point, the interrelation with others will fall easily into place. Since, presumably you want to be good at your relationships with people, you must now get a clear picture of the effect that you have on others – especially those that you are frequently in contact with.

It is now the perfect time for you to give yourself (with the help of others) a critical self assessment. In the very next chapter, I'll explain exactly how to go about getting an honest, direct, objective appraisal of your current interpersonal strengths and also those areas that need a bit of improvement.

As a certified effective thinker, it will be relatively easy for you to capitalise on your strengths and minimise the negative effects of your 'so-called' weaknesses. Once you identify a weakness or two or even three or four, I'll explain to you how to go about correcting it step by step. Effective thinkers can make any improvement they want if they develop a proper plan. They become great at dealing with other people by improving bit by bit. You'll see how easy it will be to use your effective thinking to be more assertive if you want to, to be a better risk-taker, a better negotiator, get closer to certain people, to make better presentations, to be more influential or whatever else you aim to be and you'll do this according to your own critical self assessment [programme 3].

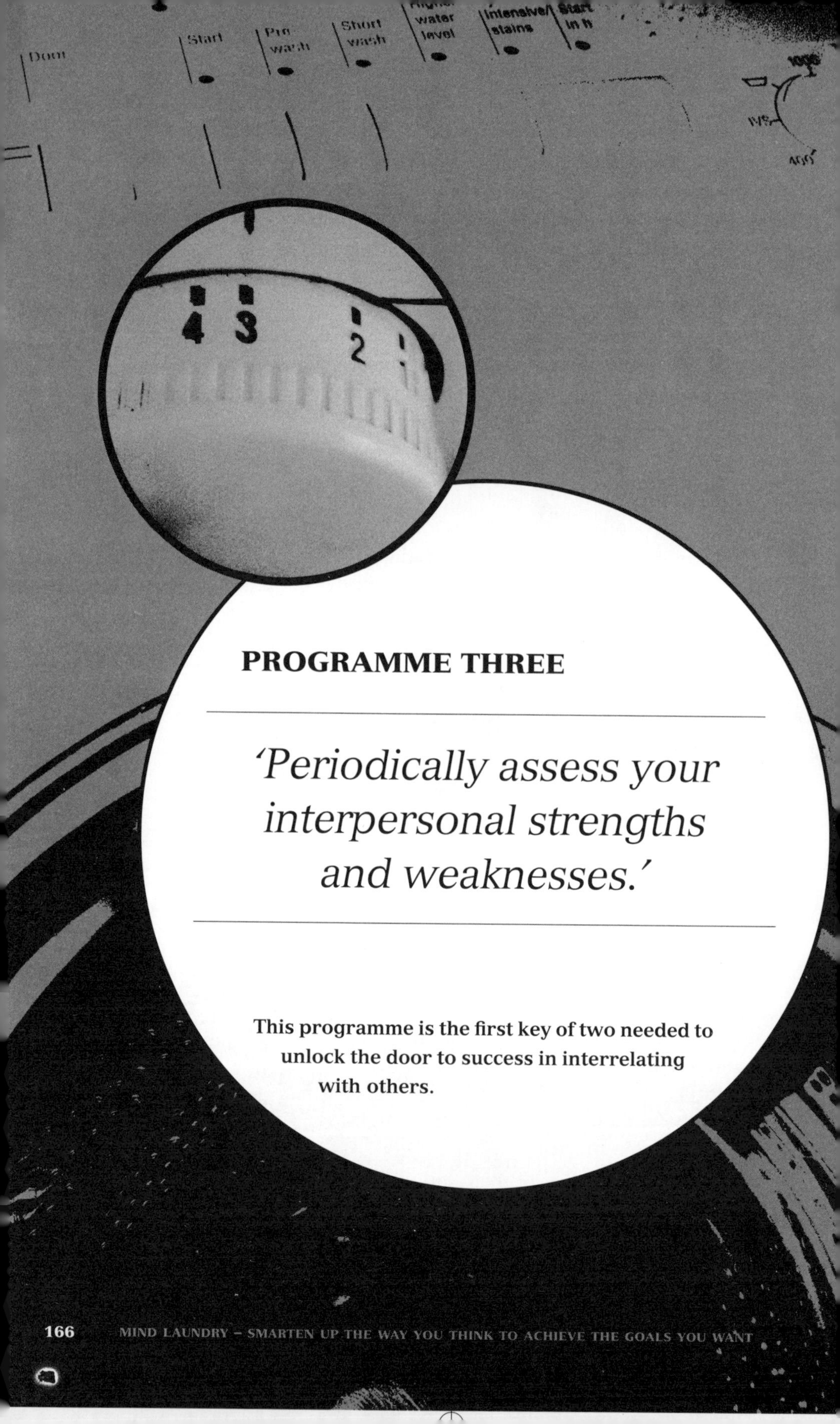

PROGRAMME THREE

'Periodically assess your interpersonal strengths and weaknesses.'

This programme is the first key of two needed to unlock the door to success in interrelating with others.

TWELVE
Analysing your effect on others

Effective thinkers know that it is important to periodically assess their personal and professional strengths if they wish to manage others. This is where programme 3 comes into use, opening the first door to successfully interrelating with others.

> **Programme 3:** Periodically assess your managerial strengths and weaknesses.

If you have decided to be good at dealing with other people, be **great** at it, it makes great sense, does it not, to have a good idea of how people perceive you?

Interpersonal communication involves two parties: yourself and the other person. The way that you see yourself is of paramount importance. With effective thinking 'installed,' you can see yourself, personally, in a way that will do a lot of good. But how do others see you?

Certainly how you see them is important, but how they see you is even more important. In this chapter, we'll explore ways for finding out how the people that you are in contact with perceive you. What is the effect that your persona, effective thinker or not, has on other people. Begin with a critical self-assessment.

Conducting your critical self-assessment

Step one:	Begin with writing down exactly how you see yourself. A personality or aptitude test or two can be helpful here.
Step two:	Next, make a prediction about how others are likely to see you.
Step three:	Then find out. Get objective feedback from relevant other people. At home, ask your partner. At work, ask your boss. Consider 360 degree feedback. Take a course. Ask people. Do whatever you can to find out the effect that your persona has on relevant others.
Step four:	Compare the view that others have of you with how you thought you would be perceived. End up with a more realistic self-picture in terms of the effect that your persona really has on others.
Step five:	Develop a realistic plan to get others to see you in a more optimal fashion.

Step one: put how you see yourself in writing

In chapter two, you invested some time clarifying your goals. There it was expected that you would take as your goal – 'the relentless pursuit of a full and satisfying life.' Now I am going to ask you be more specific in terms of your personal or professional objective(s) over the next five years. What is your main personal and/or professional goal over the next few years? Please write it in the space provided opposite.

Exercise

My main personal or professional goal over the next few years:

____

____

____

Please be sure to keep this goal in mind as you do your self-appraisal.

Below are some steps you can take in order to help you with your self-assessment:

- Personality tests, though often short on reliability and validity, can be useful in making a self-assessment. At work for example, ask your human resources director if any such instruments are available for your use. Keep in mind, that these instruments help you understand more clearly the way that you see yourself. However, these instruments are not good indicators of the way that others actually see you.
- What kind of first impression do you usually make on others? Be sure to find out by asking relevant others. First impressions are much more powerful than most of us realise. Zunin and Zunin in their book *Contact: The First Four Minutes*, studied people at cocktail parties and found out that when one person met another, they made a decision of whether to talk to each other again for the rest of their lives, in the first four minutes of conversation.

Continued over

- Do you think you are reasonably intelligent? Are you more of a critical thinker than a very sensitive and emotional person?
- Have you mastered most of the ideas regarding effective thinking, presented earlier in this book?
- Are you creative? If yes, in what ways?
- Are you more of a social person (being with people) than a person who likes to work more or less alone and with ideas?
- Do you tend to be intuitive, operating with a gut feeling rather than a need for all the facts? Or do you prefer to have most of the facts before you move into action?
- Are you the kind of person who likes to keep his or her options open, or do you prefer to have the decision made as soon as possible?
- Are you good at working with people? Why or why not?
- Are you truly motivated to be an outstanding success? Why? Why not?
- Are you generally well-organised?
- Are you a trustworthy and reliable worker? Is your word your bond?
- Are you the type of person who tends to see the job through to the very end, even when the job is difficult? Or do you tend to skip from job to job, not seeing many of them through to the very end?

- What are your six greatest interpersonal and professional strengths? What are your six main areas in need of a bit of improvement, as you see it? List them below:

My six greatest strengths

1 ____________________

2 ____________________

3 ____________________

4 ____________________

5 ____________________

6 ____________________

My six main areas in need of a bit of improvement

1 ____________________

2 ____________________

3 ____________________

4 ____________________

5 ____________________

6 ____________________

Step two

Now, before receiving concentrated feedback, ask yourself, how you think you are perceived by relevant others. Put what you anticipate, in writing below. (I believe that others will tend to see me as follows):

My main strengths

1 ______________________________

2 ______________________________

3 ______________________________

4 ______________________________

5 ______________________________

6 ______________________________

Areas in need of improvement

1 ______________________________

2 ______________________________

3 ______________________________

4 ______________________________

5 ______________________________

6 ______________________________

Step three: now find out exactly what others think of you

Get objective feedback. Clear up any blind spots that you may have. How do others really see you?

Your success with other people in your private and professional life is connected to a large extent with the subjective judgement that others have of you: especially those in close contact with you. Their perception of you has a great deal to do with your people skills. Since outstanding results in your dealings with people presumes that you can influence them, an objective analysis of your influencing capacities and the way other people see you is crucial.

One way to get this kind of necessary feedback is to take an interactive and intense programme to help you accomplish a critical self-assessment. Examine interpersonal intangibles in that setting. Experiment with and examine your present interactive style and refine and improve it – in response to the straightforward and frank feedback that you receive. Arrange, somehow, if possible, to get out of your day to day setting situation into a relaxed, informal setting with friends or out of your daily work situation with a small group of other managers and executives. Talk to each other. Discover ways in which your behaviour and attitudes affect others. In a work context, consider putting yourself and others in the capable hands of a qualified professional trainer. Cover in this training seminar (or in a strictly personal follow up with a counselling session) such things as listening, communicating, leading, handling frustration and anger, asserting yourself, facing pressures, relating to colleagues, personal openness, handling stress, perceiving, respecting other people's feelings, selling your ideas to other people, and giving and receiving constructive criticism.

In some of the business sessions that I conduct, managers from eight or nine different countries spend a week together and get to know each other very well – formally and informally and the venue is usually a small hotel away from distractions. It becomes what I call a high-yield, low-risk environment, because no-one in the seminar knows the other persons from before, nor are they from the same company. Consequently, no real politics are involved.

Daniel on the luxury of integrity

'I don't work with John. He is from a different company and another industry. There are no business politics at work during this seminar. That's not the way it is back on my regular job. So with John as well as with all the others in this seminar, I finally have the luxury of integrity. I can be perfectly honest and don't have to worry if being so honest will effect my job success.'

Therefore, we eliminate the political aspects of honest feedback. We have what I refer to as 'the luxury of integrity.' You have a very good chance of finding out, objectively, what others really think of you in such an arrangement.

After getting to know each other quite well, formally and informally, near the end of the programme we have what I call a major feedback session. Here the group (perhaps 8 to 10 others) talk *about you* as if you were not in the room. As the course director, I facilitate a discussion about the first impressions they had of you. Then the group discusses: whether or not, based on what they have got to know about you at that point, they would want you as a boss and why or why not, whether they would have you as a colleague and why or why not; a direct subordinate and why or why not; and also I have each member of the group formulate for you a word or two of honest advice that they think will do you some good.

Those who are effective thinkers take the honest feedback that they get from such a session with a grain of salt. As one effective thinker said, 'They are not talking about the real me, only the image they have of me.' However, you should know that much of what is important personal and professional life is based on image. Therefore, it is important, if you are to be a successful manager, to not only manage yourself, but also to *manage your image*.

You may not have the luxury of a free-from-politics, away-from-the-office session such as this, but even a get together with colleagues should follow the pattern and approach matters in much the same way.

In a purely personal setting, you may even be able to take the same approach with a select group of friends, or in a modified way use it to approach a partner.

OUTLINE OF FEEDBACK PROCEDURE

(Example is drawn from a business management setting)

Part one – the presentation

1 Person seeking feedback (presenter) describes main professional goal (within next few years)

2 Presents strengths (+) and areas in need of improvement (-)

3 Feedback group asks questions and asks for examples on anything that was not clear. No advice, yet.

Part two – the feedback

1 Feedback group shares individual perceptions of first impression, adjectives, animals or metaphors

2 Group reviews presenter's (+) and (-) and adds or subtracts

3 Choose as a boss? Yes/no, why or why not?

4 Accept as a boss? (Would you resign?) Yes/no, why or why not?

5 Choose as a colleague? Yes/no, why or why not?

6 Hire to work for you? Yes/no, why or why not?

7 A brief word of advice. 'You could do a little bit better if only…'

Using a standard method such as '360 degree feedback' (where all those that deal with you fill out an appraisal form) can be very useful. Or at work you can directly ask your boss for his honest, objective performance appraisal, but be sure that your boss is properly qualified to give such an appraisal. Some bosses are not very good at making such assessments. At home you could always ask your partner.

Step four: after the appraisal (regardless of the means you use), figure out what makes most sense to improve

If there is a high level of accord between the way that others see you and the way that you see yourself, you are already on the right track, but if there is a great discrepancy between how you are really affecting others, then there is some image work to be done.

If there is straight-forward feedback, you will be better able to identify those areas which you need to improve. Effective thinkers face the facts. Develop a strategy or plan to remedy any of these deficits.

This then takes us to Programme 4. Programme 4 unlocks the final door of the four doors that were guarding the entrance way to outstanding personal and professional success. Programme 4 requires that you concentrate on improving whatever it is that you have to improve to be a little better in management. Continuous self improvement, as you probably know is based on the Japanese concept of 'Kaizen.' Japanese management applies the process of improving, little by little, day by day, to the manufacture of an outstanding product. Effective thinkers do the same thing, but apply continuous improvement to making themselves better in their dealings with other people, improving day by day, bit by bit.

Figure out what area or areas it makes the most sense for you to improve. Then go about making those improvements, bit by bit. Pause and choose effective thoughts as you go along.

Improving bit by bit

- Does your performance evaluation suggest that you are insufficiently assertive? Applying programmes 1 and 2 first and then adding a few new twists to your approach with people will take care of that in no time. All this is explained in chapter 13.
- Want to know how to take the kind of risks that have maximum payoff? See chapter 14.
- Need to become a better negotiator? See chapter 15.
- Fearful of making presentations? Want to make excellent ones. See chapter 17.
- Need to improve your influencing skills? Want to have more influence over your boss, your colleagues or your direct subordinates? See chapter 18.
- Anything else? Once you master how to use effective thinking to get your mind to work for you – using it to successfully interrelate with others will fall easily into place.

PROGRAMME FOUR

'Systematically improve bit by bit.'

Areas you might wish to improve bit by bit might include for example: being assertive, taking risks, negotiating, getting closer to certain others, making presentations, or in influencing others in general.

Chapters 13 through 18 concentrate on these areas.

THIRTEEN
Being assertive, effectively

Being assertive (not overly aggressive or abrasive) as a person is an important quality. It can help you be stronger while at the same time keep others from taking undue advantage of your good nature. Effective thinkers can be just as assertive as they want to be.

A healthy sense of self-esteem combined with a few assertiveness training principles is all that you'll need to hone this important quality to the sharpness needed.

SOME EFFECTIVE THOUGHTS FOR BEING ASSERTIVE

1 You influence others, you don't really control them.

2 Be realistic in your expectations about other people's behaviour, not merely reasonable.

3 Remember, you are a chief executive officer in charge of your world, but only from the neck-up.

4 You are not your image, but you can play the image game to win.

5 People will tend to treat you the way that you teach them to treat you.

6 You are your inner identity which has within it the essential ingredients of inner calm, purpose and adventure.

You influence others

You can only influence, not control the other person. By creating a command presence, you can assert yourself, but you also need to be convincing with and without words. However, remember that you do not control how others think, feel or behave, not only are you responsible for the behaviour of others, but you are fully responsible for your own assertive behaviour, verbally and non-verbally. Assert the personal power you have, now that you have learned how to do effective thinking.

Have realistic expectations

Because you only influence and do not control others, be realistic in your expectations and you will not be disappointed. Certainly it is important that you have realistic expectations about how others operate. You can be very assertive and still not have another person act the way you had hoped they would act. Therefore, it is wise to prefer, but not to need another person to act in a certain way.

Acting assertively is a game

Play 'the assertiveness game' to win

If it pays to be assertive, then by all means act assertively. Acting assertively is just that – an act. As in all other games, it pays to play to win. As you may have noticed, most people in this world are quite insecure and if it makes sense to do so, you can take advantage of that fact. If need be, pretend that you are an assertive person, even if that is not your basic temperament. Acting assertively will have the very same effect as if that is the way you really are. Perception, when it comes to dealing with others, becomes reality.

People treat you the way that you teach them to treat you

I find this concept very useful in being assertive. If you allow yourself to be a pushover, you are teaching others to treat you that way. Teach them instead to treat you with respect and with dignity. If you are a good teacher, they will learn.

Avoid being manipulated

If you notice that someone is trying to manipulate you a bit too much, calmly call that person aside and explain to him or her that that kind of behaviour on their part is unacceptable to you. Tell them nicely to kindly refrain and thank them in advance.

- Use assertive body language in doing this.
- Don't forget direct eye contact.
- And stand tall.

If you are the type of individual that has always had a bit of trouble saying no, practice saying no. If at meetings you are asked to serve on too many committees, practice saying 'I respectfully decline', using the above guidelines. If someone persists in asking you why you decline, practice saying, 'for personal reasons.' Most persons will stop pressuring you at that point.

Assertive vs aggressive

Let's make a clear distinction between being assertive and being aggressive. Being assertive means standing up for your principles and your rights. Being assertive means taking the initiative, not simply being reactive. Being aggressive suggests going even further than merely standing up for your rights. Aggressiveness suggests imposing on the other person, sometimes a lot, sometimes just a bit.

Being labelled is not a good thing, but labelling does exist. You do not want to be labelled 'aggressive', it is better to be labelled 'assertive.'

In all cases, being 'effectively assertive' requires a sense of time and place.

When to be assertive: timing and context

Timing is everything. Ask any athlete. Ask a stockbroker – he'll tell you that the secret of getting rich is knowing when to buy and when to sell.

BE TIMELY: CARLA'S FOLLY

> Carla, as office manager, was overworked and deserved a chance to assertively 'let go,' to be irresponsible for a change. But the office party was not the ideal place for her to enjoy this release, at least not in the way that she went about it. When the music began, Carla did a dance combined with a series of gestures that made Madonna look tame. To top it all, she went over to her boss and let him have a piece of her mind. She unloaded everything that had been pent up and bothering her at work over the past year. It just was not the right time or place for these overly assertive actions. Carla was assertive all right, but effective, no.

Carla's dance at another time might have been delightful and appropriate. In just one hour of inappropriate assertiveness she had managed to jeopardise her relationships with her boss and her colleagues and her chances for advancement. Net point: don't let your assertive acts louse up aspects of your life that are of lasting importance to you.

Being assertive in the here and now

Every 'here' and 'now' occurs in a context. On one cold, blustery day recently, I spoke to an elderly man who was pumping gas at the local station. 'Freezing cold. Must be tough working outside on a day like today,' I said. 'Not really,' he said. 'I like cold weather. I really enjoy it. It's my favourite.' That's clearly a very effective attitude for him to have, considering his job. Who is to argue with him about the pleasures of freezing weather? All you need do is choose the effective thoughts that make your situation satisfying.

WHAT CAN GO WRONG, MAY GO WRONG: SO WHAT?

> Zorba the Greek, in Kazantzakis's novel, also did a memorable dance. It was eminently more effective than Carla's. The huge log-tow rig that he assertively advocated and worked so mightily and took so long to build came tumbling down in a crash. It was a tragic failure. But instead of simply reacting as a victim; instead of crying in frustration and despair, Zorba looked up to the sky, spontaneously, as if there was music coming from the heavens and created a marvellously beautiful and crazy dance with his partner. The dance integrated perfectly with Zorba's philosophy of extracting the maximum satisfaction out of life regardless of what mistakes he might have made.

Zorba tried something and failed, but then he danced. If you risk being assertive and it does not work out, it will not be a disaster.

Don't wait too long

DEFECTIVE THOUGHT

I like to play it safe. Trustworthy friends, famous brands, no side roads, only major highways. I like to know well in advance what to expect. I'm not one for surprises.

EFFECTIVE THOUGHT

I enjoy getting off the beaten path. I learn and discover when I take risks. I enjoy adventure and excitement. I enjoy risks in relationships, loving, leaving, sex, being assertive, money, telling what I feel, failing, and changing, but all in concert with a sense of inner calm and personal purpose.

You do not have to seek perfection either in yourself or in others. Proceed at your own pace, assertively, and don't wait until you've perfected what you intend to do, whether it is approaching an authority figure, taking a trip, or even telling a joke. If you wait for the perfect time to do anything, that time may never come. Sometimes it pays to act first and then analyse your action. If you're waiting until everything is 'just right' before you begin assertively writing that book or taking that trip or assertively approaching that interesting person, stop waiting. Act. Remember, regardless of what happens, you'll be able to handle it. If you fail, you will bounce back and move on towards becoming more effectively assertive the next time.

Let your hair down from time to time

'Letting go,' 'suspending critical judgement,' 'acting with abandon – letting your hair down' – all of these are forms of assertiveness. Although it is true that during some assertive actions there is an absence of critical thought, *a thought-choosing process* is still going on. You still remain *responsible* for the thoughts you choose when you are relaxed or intoxicated; but even though you are actually responsible, you can take a rest from feeling responsible. You rely on your pre-programmed intuition, instinct, habits, rather than critical thought. It is not only pleasurable but also necessary to rest your critical faculties once in a while. However, you can only do this comfortably when your instincts and habits have been trained through practice to serve your best interests (Zorba) and not your worst (Carla).

There are people who are terrified to try to dance. 'The only way that I would dance is if I had the proper training. Someday I'm going to take the lessons and really do it right.' So in the meantime they sit around and watch others 'make fools of themselves,' but it is these so-called fools who are having a good time. Those who sit on the sidelines waiting for perfection to strike can often spend an entire lifetime watching the world go by. Accepting the fact that you might not be doing something to perfection, but that you are doing the best that you know how, at that particular point in your life, is a very freeing and effective thought.

A thought for your files (*choose one*)

DEFECTIVE THOUGHT

I'm tired of playing it straight. Damn it. I'm letting go – no matter what.

EFFECTIVE THOUGHT

I'm letting go. This is a good time and place to let go.

A thought for your files (*choose one*)

DEFECTIVE THOUGHT

I'd better always be on the alert and keep trying to consciously choose my thoughts.

EFFECTIVE THOUGHT

I'm in a safe place. Good time to let go and stop being so critical and analytical. I'll just relax and trust my intuition. No need here to consciously choose effective thoughts, moment by moment.

Self-trust

In asserting yourself, it is important that you trust yourself.

PROFESSOR HOPKINS AND RICHARD

(**1**) Professor Hopkins pulled her yellowed notes from her files. They were labelled 'Lecture 21: The Romantic Period.' Professor Hopkins had been reading this very same set of notes to her weary undergraduate classes for the last ten years.

(**2**) Richard tried vainly to smile. But his stomach was tight as a drum. Why is it that he couldn't relax even in good company? His stomach was always tense. He almost had to rehearse everything in advance before he let it come out of his mouth.

The main reason these people were so non-assertive was because for one reason or another they had not learned to trust themselves. Effective thinkers know when to, and when not to, trust themselves. They know their strengths and weaknesses.

Professor Hopkins might have risked speaking more assertively and confidently to her classes if she thought, 'When I get up in front of class without notes, some of the best ideas about the Romantic Period will arrive in the foreground of my conscious mind.' Her believing that, could have made it happen. Not only would Professor Hopkins have benefited, but so would her students.

Richard, the shy one, can also be helped. He too could use effective thinking to bring himself to believe that he would no longer be overly concerned about what others are thinking about him and his actions.

Lecturing assertively: a personal experience

Many years ago, I was invited to teach a post-graduate course for the first time. I was very pleased and, naturally, I was quite anxious to do well. So in anticipation of each lecture, I prepared and prepared, even going so far as to haul a big box of books from class to class. These books (with certain places carefully marked in each of them), along with my extensive notes, were my security blanket. I had a great fear that I wouldn't have anything worthwhile to offer the graduate students if I relied primarily on my own ideas and instincts. At the conclusion of the courses, I asked the students to anonymously give my teaching an evaluation. I was astonished at how many wrote something to this effect:

> *'Dr. Kushel, the course was fine, but the reading from your notes and the books that you had marked up was quite boring after a while. I wish that you would have shared more of yourself and your actual experiences as a counsellor and therapist. The few times that you did tell us about your real-life professional experiences were the best parts of the course.*
>
> ***P... don't be afraid to be yourself. You seem to have a lot to offer.'***

Since that time I have risked being my assertive self many times, both in teaching and in my personal life. Through this process of 'risking', I have discovered many exciting aspects of myself that would have undoubtedly remained unknown and untested if I had not become sufficiently self-trusting.

PRISONER FARRELL

> Farrell, an extremely tense 43 year old marketing director, came to me for consultation. Because he had established a marvellous reputation for being highly reliable and competent, he had become trapped. Many people (his boss and colleagues alike) looked to him for advice, and he was flattered. 'One thing about me,' he said, 'people know I'm good at what I do.' It was only after Farrell came to realise that the pressure of keeping an excellent reputation was taking its toll on his insides, on his nerves, that he began to choose more effective thoughts. 'I'm not my reputation,' he later came to say to himself. 'My reputation is only an image. People will have to learn to accept me for being me – and the me that I am is far from perfect.' When Farrell decided for himself that he would settle for a lesser reputation, the strain upon his nervous system eased considerably. Interestingly, when he let up on himself, his work somehow improved, even though he wasn't trying nearly as hard.

In my own case, I may seem unreliable to those who don't really know me. After all, I know no thought is unthinkable. Who knows – if it makes sense to me, I might just take off cross country. I do not allow myself to be a mere prisoner of any situation. I might even decide to walk out in the middle of a meeting and be alone for a while. The freedom that such thinking affords me is critical to my inner liberation. Since I am confident that I can handle any 'now,' any consequences of my actions, I feel loose and assertive and fundamentally I am more myself and therefore more reliable and stable.

A thought for your files (*choose one*)

DEFECTIVE THOUGHT

You can always count on me, no matter what. I'm 'good old reliable.'

EFFECTIVE THOUGHT

Please never, under any circumstances, take me for granted. Unless you really know me, you might be surprised by my next act.

Stand up for your rights

If you are too often taken advantage of, stand up for yourself. It might not, sometimes, be a bad idea to get one of your T-shirts emblazoned with the warning, 'Don't take me for granted.' Those who love you (that is, really listen to and care for you on your own terms) will not be confused because they will know 'where you're coming from.' The people who don't really listen to and care for you all that much might sometimes think you are unreliable.

Resiliency

The ability to bounce back after you've made a mistake is a crucial element in living. You are bound to make human mistakes. Bouncing back confidently from these errors is essential. While Carla made a fool of herself by dancing uninhibitedly at the office party, even though she may have lost points on the job, her life still goes on. She can learn from her mistake. Certainly Carla, even though she risked imperfectly, is more alive than Professor Hopkins, who never chanced speaking to her students without her rusty, outdated notes. To risk assertively and louse up is still better than never to have risked at all.

A thought for your files (*choose one*)

DEFECTIVE THOUGHT

I fouled up. I'm just no good. I should never have said what I was thinking. I'll never be able to get back on track.

EFFECTIVE THOUGHT

I made a mistake. But, that's OK. I'm back 100 per cent back on track as of this very moment. Feels good to be on course.

FOURTEEN
Risking, effectively

Being effectively assertive and taking risks go hand in hand. It was Lord Halifax who said, 'He that leaveth nothing to chance will do few things ill, but he will do very few things.'

When Marc took the receiver off the hook, his heart began to pound like that of an adolescent. He could hardly breathe. 'This is too much,' he thought. He put down the receiver, took a handkerchief from his pocket, and wiped the clammy sweat from his forehead and both palms. 'Imagine,' he thought, 'a grown man afraid to make a call, to risk failure, to experience rejection.'

Alice used to enjoy her work, but now more and more was being piled on her already overloaded desk. It seemed as if there was no way out. She was tired of being 'dumped on' literally and figuratively, but she just didn't seem able to muster up the courage to put a stop to it.

'Look at this awful traffic jam,' Edward lamented. For years now, he had been fantasising a time when he would turn his car off the crowded motorway some morning and not show up for work. He dreamed of heading for the beach, taking a swim, wandering carefree along the shore. But no. Good old reliable Edward. They could always count on good old Edward, veritable prisoner of his own reliable reputation.

Taking risks is an integral part of a self-responsible way of life. The synergy of calm, purpose, and adventure enables one to engage in and enjoy risk-taking ventures with little of the anxiety that most other people experience in similar circumstances. Effective thinkers generally take a low-tension approach to most risking while other types of people often find risk-taking quite draining. Consequently, effective thinkers are able to conserve their energy for the times when it may actually be needed.

Life with surprise in it has zest. Perhaps that is one of the reasons why reading the morning newspaper remains such a popular pastime. People are curious to see if something new has happened in the world overnight, but this is often insufficient. There can be a wearisome sameness in the headlines, the stock market, even the football results. Vicarious excitement, though helpful, is not enough. People yearn for more adventure in their lives, but day-after-day routine is all they often have.

Some kinds of risks might seem well worth taking. Others, quite foolish, even stupid. Mindless, thrill-seeking behaviour might serve as an occasional respite from responsible living. However, the kinds of risk taking that we will focus upon in this chapter will be of a more purposeful nature. We will examine calculated risks that tend to lead toward greater inner liberation, a more satisfying personal existence.

THE FOUR ESSENTIAL STEPS TOWARD EFFECTIVE RISK TAKING

Effective risk taking requires that the prospective risk taker go through four necessary steps usually, but not always, in this sequence:

1. Assess the prospects for success.
2. Imagine handling effectively the worst that could possibly happen in the event of failure.
3. Imagine completing the risk in ideal fashion.
4. Keeping the positive fantasy in mind, let go, act and enjoy.

Assessing the prospects for success

Even risks that are taken on short notice require forethought. Check out the situation in advance as soon as possible. Have some sense of the odds you face. All risks should be calculated to some extent. Decide if the reward involved seems worth the risk involved. If it does, then proceed to step two.

Imagining that you are handling effectively the worst that could happen in the event of failure

Can you handle the prospect of failure? Can you afford to lose? Sometimes an individual becomes aware that the stakes in case of loss are overwhelming. For example if you were to fail to pass a speeding car on a narrow highway and a crash proved inevitable, the loss would be considerable – perhaps your life and even the lives of others. However, given sufficient space and time, you might venture the risk. Failure, in this instance, would be irreconcilable and unconscionable.

However, with a great number of other risks, the ways of dealing with the possibility of failure are multifold. It is often possible to invent a large number of effective approaches for dealing with failure. If, for example, one were to approach a new prospective customer and attempt to sell him a product, imagine the worst that could happen. If the advances were ignored, would the risk taker pass out? Would he cry? In either case, the risk taker will survive. If he passes out in his imagination, what then? He can imagine getting up off the ground, when he regains consciousness and going about his business. In fact anything that he imagines, short of bodily harm, can be handled in the mind's eye if approached creatively.

This step is one that is often omitted by those who too quickly urge people to risk by thinking only positive thoughts. Then the possibility of failure seems to lurk ominously in the back of the risk taker's mind and is often blown far out of proportion to the risk taker's capacity to handle it. It is precisely at this stage that effective thinkers are most inventive and it is this process, thinking through the possibility of failure, that allows them to engage in low-tension risking when others experience great anxiety in the same situation.

Imagining completing the risk in ideal fashion

Our images serve as our self-fulfilling prophecies. Therefore, it is worthwhile for the risk taker to take the time to imagine a vivid picture of completing the task in an ideal fashion. This takes practice and concentration, but the benefits derived are well worth the effort. Some do this quite instinctively. Recently, the world's high-jump record was broken by a young man who attested that he saw in his mind's eye a vivid picture of himself successfully jumping over the crossbar – moments before he turned it into an actuality.

Keeping the picture of success clearly in mind, let go, act and enjoy

Keeping the successful picture clearly in mind, let go of everything else. Let go of appraising. It's too late for that now. Let go of failing. It's far too late to think of any of that now. Let go of everything except the picture of yourself succeeding. At this moment you are really doing it. You are acting. R-I-S-K. You give to this venture just what is needed. You have what it takes. You are enjoying. You have risked.

Application

It is an important business meeting (or maybe an important personal decision time – as in buying a house). It's your last chance to close the deal. If your offer is accepted, you'll make the sale. If not, you lose everything. Tension. Appraising the risk. Not too much choice here. You're already involved in the deal, and you probably are not going to choose to walk out of the office. However, the real question of risk centres around whether you should make a strong, bold offer, trying for a winner, or should you play it safely with a soft sell? You evaluate your opponent and decide that you can reasonably risk going for broke since your offer is likely to be irresistible and you think that move will push him into acceptance.

Thinking through the worst. All that can happen to you, you figure, is that you could lose the sale. That is a lot, but you also figure that you won't be destroyed if you lose. Oh, your opponent might go elsewhere and you might also berate yourself for a short time, but in no case does missing this sale mean total disaster. You find this realisation quite comforting. So, you think, calming yourself, 'All this isn't quite as bad as it seemed at first.' If you can survive the worst that you can imagine, then there is little to really worry about.

Imagining a beautiful, strong offer that your opponent cannot resist. You win. You fix this very positive image of making this marvellous deal clearly in your mind's eye. You can almost taste it.

Holding on clearly to the picture of success imprinted in your mind (an irresistible offer), you move into action. You let go of all reservation, all appraising, all fear. You act out the image in your mind's eye. You act. You R-I-S-K. You give just what it takes, no more, no less and you enjoy the excitement of the risk.

Good going. I hope that it went as you hoped. If you fully concentrated and applied these four steps exactly as described, your chances for success were excellent.

Low-tension risking

There are occasions when nothing can adequately reduce the tension of a particular risk, such as when the odds are really against you and the goal is of special importance. However, there are thoughts you can choose that can make even the most intimidating of risks less frightening. The train of thought that Max, an effective thinker, employed illustrates this.

Max, in his early thirties, married, with two small children, sought counselling because he had very little confidence in himself even though he was employed as an office manager for a large insurance company and appeared to those who didn't know him well to be 'up and coming.'

Asking for a raise can be extremely nerve-wracking, especially if your colleagues have warned you that the boss doesn't like to be pressed and has been known to fire employees for less. When jobs are scarce and one has a wife and two young children depending upon the pay cheques, it is even more difficult.

Max did risk asking for a raise; the following reflects the self-managing line of thought he finally developed to minimise his anxiety.

MAX'S LINE OF THOUGHT FOR RISKING

> 'No, I didn't get very uptight asking for the raise. First of all, I figured out that they [the company] had enough money in the till so that they could afford to give me a justified increase. I was aware that they knew damn well that I was doing good work. So I personally figured that my prospects were quite good regardless of what the crowd said.
>
> 'Secondly, the way I figured it, what's the worst thing that could happen to me if the boss didn't like my asking? Fire me? Right! He definitely wouldn't hit me. I knew that he couldn't put me in jail. The worst that he could do was fire me. So then I figured, okay, so if he fires me, what then? I thought about that for quite a while.

'The way I've come to feel about myself these days is that although I really like working there, it's not the only job that I can do in order to make a living. Hell, if I had to, I believe that I could do landscaping, selling, even factory work. So with that in mind, I said to myself, 'Max, what have you got to be scared of?' However, then I thought of Cheryl and the kids. What about them? After all, they count on my pay cheque every two weeks, and I wouldn't want to let them down by losing this job.

'So here's the way that I handled that. I said to myself, 'Max, Cheryl loves you for what you are, not for the fact that you're a big-deal office manager and bringing home a cheque every two weeks. If she doesn't really love you for what you are, then this is as good a time as ever to find out. So I figured, I'm not afraid of the truth; whatever the truth is, I can handle it. This led me to the conclusion that the risk of asking for the raise could only lead toward a clearer picture of reality. It would help me get closer to the truth about my marriage possibly, and I was certainly bound to find out whether I really have any kind of future with this company. Anyhow, asking was my goal. I figured I had a fighting chance. If I didn't get it, I could still handle any of the consequences. So, I went in, and I asked. And I got it.'

Analysis of Max's thinking

Max's risk-taking freed him to put into effect other self-managing concepts. The playing of roles as compared to actually doing a job was a central concept in his line of thought. Max was clearly able to tell the difference between playing roles and real action. He alluded to his comprehension of this concept when he said, 'They knew damn well that I was doing good work.' Max believed that he was actually doing a job for the company rather than merely playing a role.

Playing a role is similar to being in a play or show. You look as if you are real, but you are actually pretending. Many people confuse role-playing with the real thing. Self-managed people do not. Max also concerned himself with this important principle when he reflected on his wife, Cheryl. 'If she doesn't love me for what I am, then this is as good a time as ever to find out.' If Cheryl was simply playing the role of wife and lover, he would find this out if his risk-taking venture were to fail. Max perceived Cheryl as a true friend and lover, not simply a person playing the conventional role of wife and he was willing to find out if his perceptions were correct. He was not limited to basing his thoughts only on illusion, but on actual behaviour.

Effective thinkers are not above playing roles, but they also do jobs and they clearly know the difference between the two. They see role-playing for what it is and do not take 'playing' seriously. They take the jobs they (and other people) do, quite seriously, because doing a job is real and role-playing is not.

Imagine a man with a white coat and a stethoscope. He stands ominously in front of you, dangling his stethoscope. He says, 'I'm a physician, an important physician.' 'Great,' you say, 'but can you heal people? What's your healing average?' He replies, 'Can't you see? This is a stethoscope, and a doctor's coat. I'm a doctor!' 'Yes,' you respond, calmly, 'but can you heal? What's your batting average?' And the man in the doctor's outfit walks away, disgusted with you.

There are many people walking around with the trappings of a role who cannot perform at all when it comes to a test. I once knew a person who looked as if he would be an excellent football coach. He was tall and strong. He looked athletic and he could bluff his way in talk about football. He looked the part – direct from central casting – but in truth, he would have been a terrible coach. He, in reality, knew practically nothing about the game and never even played it.

All of us are required by society to play a variety of roles each day and there is nothing inherently wrong with that, as long as we don't confuse roles with reality.

Max's reference to his new attitude was clarified by his subsequent comments. He confided to me that his father had dominated him for most of his life and that he had only recently confronted his father about that fact. After the blow-up, Max said he felt emancipated from needing to please his father, the way he had for so long. This difficult and painful experience led Max to a low period in which he succeeded in redefining himself in his current fashion.

Many of the other people that I have come to identify as effective thinkers noted that they also experienced a similar period of despair in which they learned to develop a more effective definition of themselves. Such a period of despair can be the result of taking a risk and not succeeding, but what separates self managed people from the rest is that they bounce back and are inspired to redefine themselves. Very often when people survive a difficult period they emerge all the stronger, and the resources and new perspectives developed out of such a situation can often have long-lasting positive effects.

The degree of caring is another factor worth considering here. Max was certainly a caring person, even if he appeared to others to have 'nerves of steel.' He cared about his wife and his children. He cared about his job. He cared about getting a raise. And, he also cared about himself. Caring about oneself is often misconstrued as selfishness. Self-care is not the same as selfishness. Selfishness suggests caring about yourself regardless of what happens to other persons. Self-managing people are not selfish, but do exercise a great deal of self-care. They identify with all of mankind, yet they realise that if they are not in pretty good shape, they will have very little of consequence that they can offer others.

Not caring about what others think or do is usually a glib simplification. 'I don't care,' can usually be more accurately translated, 'I don't care as much about ________________ as I do about ________________ or, ________________ but I care more about ________________ than I do about ________________ or ________________.'

Max cared about his job, about his wife and children, about the raise, but it was all a matter of degree. The fact that self-managed persons have ordered their lives' priorities prepares them for situations such as this.

There are risks that are not consciously viewed as risks. For example, a person is sometimes thought of as very independent when in reality he/she is just afraid to ask for help. 'Independent' is often a cover for fear of risking rejection or looking foolish.

Donna, another effective thinker and risk taker, looked at asking for help this way: 'When I ask if I can take on a new job, my boss can always say no if she wants to. I won't get upset if she says no. In fact I deeply feel that she is entitled to say 'no' if that's what she wants to say. I don't feel as if I can take responsibility for her situation any more than I can expect that she can take responsibility for mine. So I went over to see her yesterday and said, 'Linda, can I move into the marketing division for the experience? Okay?' Well, she looked at me in a funny way, then kind of reluctantly she gave me the go-ahead sign. I really appreciated her giving me that opportunity. I really wanted it and I knew that I would be glad to do the same for her if the situation were reversed. I honestly feel that she's entitled to make her own decision. People are often glad to help out if you just ask. Now don't get me wrong. I'm not out to make a pest of myself or use other people. I value people too much for that. The way I look at it, when I ask them for help, in a way, I'm giving them a chance to find out more about themselves and what they really feel. I just hope that they can be honest with me.'

Men who act overly macho are often afraid of risking to ask for help. So are students who are afraid to raise their hands in class and ask about something that they do not quite understand. 'Everyone will find out that I'm stupid.' Ted, an 18 year old high school student and former client, developed an interesting rationale for asking questions: 'Many of my friends are so concerned with how they look that they actually pretend that they know what is going on in science class. They almost never ask questions, even when they don't know what Mr. Kaufman is talking about. It seems that I'm always the one. So when Kaufman explains something and he uses a few words that I've never heard before, my hand goes up. Everyone else is just sitting there pretending that they know what it is that he's talking about. So Kaufman gives me that big fisheye of his – and then he clarifies what it is that he's talking about. Hell, I just want to learn science; I'm not into impressing Kaufman. Then after class, it happens every time, somebody will come up to me and say, 'Boy, I didn't understand that either, but am I glad that it was you that asked him to explain it.' Listen, that's the way a lot of people are, I know it, but I can't take responsibility for them. It's hard enough just taking responsibility for myself.'

Mistaken attitudes toward risk-takers sometimes inhibit those who should know better from doing what is in their best interest in the long run. The self-managed approach to risk-taking sometimes requires that we discount popular opinion in favour of effective thinking.

Worthy risks

Effective thinkers sometimes do engage in high-tension risks, but then you can be sure that the risks are worthwhile. An executive undertakes a risky project. He/she faces problems that might never have had to be faced if he/she hadn't tried something foreign, something new and risky.

Reaching out beyond familiar and established boundaries in any area can often be an intensive risk-taking venture but a highly worthwhile act. Enjoy. Succeed.

The cases and lines of thought demonstrate how the degree of tension common to many risk-taking situations can be very much reduced or even eliminated entirely. Max chose a series of thoughts for himself that not only led to attaining a raise, but kept him free from the trap of taking roles that he 'played' too seriously. He turned a potentially nerve-wracking experience into another self-managed event in his life.

Through the process of effective risk-taking, coupled with creative self-managing lines of thought, a person can really enjoy the challenge of life.

FIFTEEN
Negotiating, effectively

Effective thinkers know how to negotiate in life and the game of business, in the games that involve finance, business tactics and strategy, achieving power and in getting ahead, but they never, even for a moment, forget that they are playing the negotiation game. Since it is a game, why not play it to win? In fact, in keeping with their commitment to have a full life, but not at the expense of others, why not negotiate – win/win. I win, and you win too. Not I win, but you lose and certainly not I lose, but you win – or as some foolish people do – lose/lose. Effective thinkers go out of their way to see that their so-called 'opponent' gets fair treatment in any negotiation and makes appropriate gains as well. In a sale, they negotiate a low, but fair, price and win, but see that the person that they buy from still makes a living, gets adequate value from the transaction and makes an appropriate gain as well.

WIN/WIN

> Effective thinker Betty Mace: 'Here at the hospital there are five different departments that are competing with each other for a share of the hospital budget. I've figured out how to organise all five departments into a winning coalition. What I did was to find the mutual needs of all the departments and together we focused on our common objectives. As a hospital administrator, I need to go for win/win or the patients end up the biggest loser. After all, it's because of the patients that we're here.'

SOME 'NEGOTIATION GAME' GROUND RULES

Rule 1	Avoid, if at all possible an either/or dichotomy. Find a third way – win/win.
Rule 2	Find common ground with your opponent.
Rule 3	Figure out how getting what you want will also help your adversary.
Rule 4	Privately, think of your so-called opponent, not as an adversary, but as a prospective win/win partner.
Rule 5	Negotiate from a position of perceived strength. Remember – 'perception is reality.'

Life is serious, business is a game

Effective thinkers know how to play the interesting games negotiating for money and getting ahead in business, as well as the infinitely more serious business of life. They negotiate in the game of business, but recognise the difference between life and business. They intend to win at both, but make a clear differentiation between the two, never taking business so seriously that they spoil their lives.

Of course, the one thing effective thinkers take very seriously is their hidden identity, with its built-in elements of inner calm, purpose, and adventure. 'I'm determined to have calm, purpose, and adventure in my life, no matter what,' they say.

As a result, their top priority goal, 'to have a very satisfying personal and professional life' is never compromised. Negotiating for a raise, or for closing a business deal, or for attaining a bigger and/or better job, are areas where they have fun and adventure, in keeping with one of their important life values. Effective thinkers achieve their material goals with relative ease.

They appreciate that negotiating for making money, for getting promoted, or making deals is a game that is not under their total control. They know that external results cannot be guaranteed, that only inner results can. Therefore, they do not take external results seriously as their inner results and because they always see negotiating with another person as a game, they take off much of the pressure. Paradoxically, they often achieve their external result because they did not try too hard.

Use your image to your advantage

Effective thinker Marlene Jason: 'Please don't let anyone know. If the people back at my company ever found out how lightly I take my job, they'd be let down. They enjoy thinking of me as a workaholic. You see, my game plan calls for me to act earnestly, as if everything that happens within the company really matters. So sometimes when things go wrong, I feign worry and upset. They love it. Sometimes I act angry just to get my people up and moving. Acting angry can be productive, but really being angry usually makes very little sense. Deep down, I never forget that there are many, many more important things in this world than the production of high quality widgets and the making of profits. This world will be here long after the company, its products and I, have ceased to exist.'

REMEMBER 'P-I-T'

P = Power	Know what you want. Power means getting what you want.
I = Information	Get all the information you can. Learn all you can about your opponent's needs, true desires and limits. Know how desperate your opposition is and act accordingly.
T = Time	Make time your ally.

Power is 'getting what you want'

Effective thinker: 'Power to me means getting what I want, or at least getting what I want done by somebody else. That's all that power is. Consequently, when I get what I want, I feel powerful. However, if I don't seem to be making progress toward getting what I want, then I feel powerless. What can be even worse than getting nothing is getting something I never really ever wanted in the first place. That's why I am always clear to myself as to what I'm really after. I'm very likely to get it.'

PERCEIVED POWER IS REAL POWER

Situation: you do not have enough authority to carry out your extensive job responsibilities.

The choice is yours (*choose one*)

DEFECTIVE THOUGHT

My power comes essentially from the authority attributed to my position in the organisational structure. I've been extremely short-changed. I'm very handicapped.

EFFECTIVE THOUGHT

Most of my power is personal power. My power over others comes essentially from my awareness of other people's self-interests. Therefore, I have to care about what other people want. Then I serve their interests to the extent that I can. I manage this job effectively, while at the same time do whatever I have to do to get more official authority from the company to carry out my responsibilities even more effectively. I'm never a victim.

Information: find out what your opposition really wants

It's the people who don't know what they really want who are the most difficult for effective thinkers to handle. Effective thinker: 'Once I know what somebody is after, I can readily manage him/her but if he/she is confused, if he/she doesn't know his own mind, then I have to create goals for him/her. Confused people are the most difficult for me. It's hard to know what they are after, so they're difficult to manage.'

Make time your ally

If you have time and the opposition has less of it, that is always to your advantage. If the deadline is in your favour, you will have less pressure on you to come to an agreement than does your opposition. Moreover, if you get your opposition to invest a lot of time, your chances of having the opposition come to see things your way improve considerably.

GRACE UNDER PRESSURE

> The Grace Company wanted to buy a certain piece of property. They negotiated off and on for it with the Town Property Company for over five years. Grace Company *appeared* to be in no rush, but the Town Property Company felt that it had invested a lot of its valuable time trying to make the sale to Grace Company. When Grace finally made a low offer, Town Property took it because they felt they had already wasted too much time on trying to make this particular sale.

Negotiating with bosses and others

Effective thinkers use their negotiation skills *to get what they want* from their bosses, their subordinates, their peers, their spouses, and even from their children. Effective thinker: 'I need to work with and through people in my business. Therefore, I always try to find people who have the special talent to do the particular job that I need to get done.

Getting what you want from a negotiation with other people is a matter of finding out what they want and then putting yourself in the position to get it for them. Most intimate friends want someone who really cares for them, listens to them and appreciates them on their own terms. They thrive on such a friend's caring relationship. Since truly successful managers know to listen deeply to other people when appropriate, they easily build excellent, warm, close relationships with selected individuals, especially family and one or two close friends.

All people are motivated out of self interest

Effective thinkers: 'Since all people are motivated primarily by their own self interests, I make it my business to find out what their interests are. Then I set it up so that I'm viewed as the one who can help them get what they want. If they see me as that somebody who controls them getting what they want, I usually have them under my influence. That's how I get power. In this business (films) most of the people in it are in it for fame and fortune and I'm powerful, only because these people see me as the gatekeeper, who presides over whether they get their share of fame and fortune or not. I enjoy this business for what it is, just a game. If I ever took it seriously, I couldn't last in it.'

Negotiating with one's boss

Effective thinker: 'My boss is motivated out of his own self interests, just like me, just like anybody else. So I sat down one day and I said to myself: 'Neil, what does that crazy boss of yours really want?' Then I answered, 'He wants the very same things that you want from your subordinates. He wants total loyalty from you. He wants somebody whom he can unconditionally trust. He also wants plenty of recognition from his boss.' Every boss has a boss, even mine. Sure I'm the managing director of this company, but even I have five or six bosses. I report to the CEO and even he reports to the chairman of the board. Accountability never stops. My boss only wants to make a good impression on his boss. So since I want to get what I want out of my boss, I just make damned sure that he gets plenty of credit for whatever I do that is good. I always make it clear to him that I am totally loyal to his interests. He respects me for that. I've learned a few things over the years, much of it the hard way. I've not become the head of this operation out of nowhere.'

Negotiating with one's direct subordinates

Effective thinker Joan Drew explains *how she gets what she wants* from her direct subordinates. 'I want loyalty and a good day's work out of my staff. Therefore, it's necessary for me to identify with what they want from me and get it for them. My workers, more than anything else, want to be treated fairly, with respect and appreciation. Fairness is their biggest issue. As the boss, I'm a parental figure and, therefore, I always treat 'my people' fairly and equally. They appreciate that and do a great job for me, but if I'm ever unfair, or even perceived as being unfair, watch out!'

Joan Drew: 'I have a long-standing policy to reprimand in private and always commend in public. All people need and want dignity and I give it to them. In turn, I get done what I want to get done!'

Negotiating with one's colleagues

If you find out what your colleagues really want and get it for them, you'll probably have excellent peer relationships at work. Colleagues might undercut you if they find you too threatening. What colleagues often want from you is a simple sense that you won't undermine them, threaten their turf, or 'mess' with company job norms. If you're on a fast-track, you might be resented for spoiling the norms. The best advice, here, is to go easy! Keep a relatively low profile with colleagues and be sure never to brag. All people are interested in their own progress. To the extent that you can be helpful and share good ideas, you'll be appreciated.

Have a game plan

Effective thinkers negotiate with a game plan in mind. It sometimes appears at first glance that they have lost, only to find out later that they have won. The prize that is on display is not always the one that they are really after. Effective thinking managers have a way of feeling victorious, no matter what.

Effective thinkers do what works to meet their negotiating objective.

Exercise

Below are some situations that require some negotiating. What tactics would you recommend for each of the following?

- While travelling together to a meeting, your boss asks you to tell him confidentially what you really think of him, that he won't hold anything against you. All he wants is your honest opinion. You think he is quite overbearing at meetings. Should you tell him?
- Your colleague wants credit for the sale that you made. He makes claim to the sale in front of the boss.
- You are trying to beat out the competition in closing a deal. The competition has more experience in this particular enterprise. What is your strong card. How do you play it?
- You hope to get promoted but you have insufficient visibility in your present role. What can you do to get a higher profile?

SIXTEEN
Presenting, effectively

In making any presentation, the management of yourself is, of course, the single most critical factor. It is a fact that the greatest fear of most human beings is not the fear of death but rather, the fear of public speaking. The effective thinking methodology, and especially the rapid self-hypnosis technique that I explained earlier, provides you with all that you need to know to manage yourself when making any presentation.

However, in addition, what I am about to explain here about managing both your material and your audience will give you even more self-confidence and you will be bound to be, if you are not already, an excellent presenter, regardless of the situation.

MANAGING TO PRESENT

1 Manage yourself

2 Then manage your material

3 And then manage your audience

Manage yourself through effective thinking

Everything we've discussed so far can help you manage yourself for making a successful presentation. Use your inner metaphor to give you inner calm. Use rapid self-hypnosis to prepare yourself in advance. Follow the guidelines presented when we discussed assertiveness, self confidence, and risk taking.

Some general guidelines and effective thoughts appropriate for making presentations

1. You'd worry a whole lot less about what other people (the audience) are thinking of you if only you knew how rarely they did.
2. Don't sweat over the small stuff. (The speech that you are giving) P.S. It's all small stuff.
3. People (the audience) will treat you the way you teach them to treat you.
4. I want to give an excellent speech, not a perfect one.
5. This too shall pass.
6. The best is yet to come.
7. These people love me.
8. I'm bearing gifts to bring to these people.
9. I prefer to give a great talk, I don't need to.
10. This talk is a project, not a problem.
11. Be realistic about the objectives and success of this talk, not merely reasonable.
12. It's not the real me that is being judged during this talk, just my image.
13. Public speaking is just a game, play the game to win.
14. I did this before, so I can do it again.

15 Modulate your voice. A deeper resonant tone generally commands more respect.

16 Use self-confident body language. Create a command presence.

17 Dress for success.

18 Create a warm tone.

Managing your material

In order to manage your material, you need to know how to break it down and organise it so that your audience will appreciate your message. That's where the rule of three in public speaking truly comes into play. Keep things uncomplicated. There's the rule of K-I-S-S. 'Keep it simple, stupid.'

The rule of three

People can read a list of things, but as a speaker, you cannot realistically expect your audience to remember a laundry list.

Keep your list of anything, if at all possible, to three or less. I call this 'the rule of three.'

Notice 'The Rule Of Three' in the following:

- Above Average, Average, Below Average
- The Tall, the Medium and the Short
- The Past, the Present and the Future
- The Executive, The Judiciary and The Legislative
- It is as easy as 'ABC'
- Father, Son and Holy Ghost (the Trinity or Holy rule of three!)
- Beginning, Middle, End
- Good, Fair, Poor
- The Good, the Bad and the Ugly

- Hop, Skip and Jump
- On your marks, get set, go
- I came, I saw, I conquered

The rule of three also applies to learning how to make effective presentations and I'll discuss each of the following as we go along.

> **All speaking is either to persuade, or to inform, or to entertain. Or a combination of these three.**

Remember the letters and word: P-I-E. Persuade, inform or entertain. One or more of these three cover all possible purposes of a presentation. And if you can be entertaining as you persuade or inform, then your talk is bound to be successful.

Again, be sure not to overwhelm your audience with too many details. Adhere as much as possible to the rule of three. Never have a 'laundry list' of 10 or 20 items or more as part of any presentation.

Additional tips

- Brainstorm on a piece of paper, using your own shorthand, all the ideas you can think of off the top of your head regarding the chosen subject.
- Then pick five of your best ideas. Organise these five ideas in a system. For example, chronological, or front, middle, rear, or large, medium and small.
- Then give your talk a title. The title you give to your talk helps you to settle on a theme or a point of view.

In order to prepare your material follow this procedure

First, tell them what you are going to tell them, but don't tell everything – just a preview – enough to whet the appetite of the audience for your subject. Prepare an opening that will attract attention. Consider using a prop as a focal point. Use appropriate visual aids. Then after you have told them, make a summary, but only of a few of the highlights, not everything. Make your closing statement tie in with your theme (your title).

Organise your talk as follows

1 First, tell them what you are going to tell them.

2 Then tell them.

3 Then wrap it all up by telling them what it was that you told them.

Think of yourself as a tour guide taking a group of tourists on an interesting journey. Open by giving a bit of a preface on what you are going to say. In your opening, provide your fellow passengers (the listeners) with a road map so that they have a sense of where you are taking them. Then take them on your presentational journey, pointing out the sights as you go. At the end of the trip review a few of the highlights, so that they will leave with a good taste in their mouth.

Some notes about visuals

1 Use clear visuals. Keep them uncomplicated. Have only three ideas or less on each overhead or slide.

2 Don't talk to the visual aid. Talk to your audience.

3 Practice using your visuals in advance.

Managing your audience

Remind yourself that for the most part, the audience really wants you to do well. Remind yourself that audiences get tired of listening to even the best of speakers. It is always better to leave them asking for a bit more, than to have presented too long.

If heckled do not display sarcasm or being short-tempered, even if you are right. It won't be effective. Instead, keep your wits about you and project a calm bearing.

I use pairings (dyads) or triads or organise small syndicates or'buzz groups' and use them to keep the audience actively involved in some of my longer presentations. Keep your audience actively involved. If you are making a long presentation, create an exercise that has them leave their seats to participate.

Please get out of your seat

Ask your audience to rate (for example) their level of trust for the human species on a scale from 1 (low) to 4 (high). Then after they have made their personal rating, have them go to one of the four corners of the room that corresponds to the number that they have selected for their rating. In that section of the room they will meet others that are like minded about their trust for the human species. Have them pair up and talk about what trust means to them, and why they chose their particular rating. After this exercise, have them return to their seats and open up a general discussion about trust, or whatever topic you decided to rate.

Tips for managing your audience

1. Have friendly eye contact with various parts of the audience, not just to one side or another.
2. Mingle a bit with some members of the audience in advance for them to warm to you.
3. Move a bit when you are speaking, but not as a distraction. Don't be an automatic prisoner of the podium.
4. Assume that you are bearing gifts for the audience. Find a friendly face or two and be responsive.
5. Feel as if the members of the audience are guests in your home. Make them comfortable.
6. Speak loudly enough so that those in the back row can definitely hear you.
7. Don't talk too long. Break up your talk, if possible, with syndicate/buzz sessions, questions and answers, dyads and triads.

Adhere to the 3 Bs of public speaking

1. Be Interesting
2. Be Brief
3. Be Seated.

SEVENTEEN

A final word on influencing others, effectively

Repetition, as you know, is the mother of skill. As mentioned many times in this section of the book, there is a subtle, but extremely important distinction that must be made between *influence* and *control*. In order to move ahead in the corporate world, effective thinkers have learned how to excel in influencing others. The one effective thought that produces so much job success for them is: 'influence others, don't try to control them.'

Let us discuss in greater detail, the distinction between influence and control.

Influence vs control

Loretta Reese: 'One of my salesmen was consistently late for meetings. I called him in, but instead of reprimanding him, I explained that he might be doing himself and the company a disservice. I certainly had enough clout to influence him to be on time. All I had to do was point out the facts of the situation to him and let him figure out the rest for himself.'

Effective thinkers give their staff sufficient rope to manage their own lives – to make their own mistakes, or to create their own successes. They are quick to admit that they are *never* in charge of the thoughts that another person chooses to think. They, more than most others, appreciate that if an individual is able to choose any thought he wants to, no matter what the circumstance, then that person is also responsible for the way he or she feels or how that person behaves. They appreciate that there's no possible way at all, short of physical force, that one individual can *truly control* another. All that one person can do about another's thought-choice is to influence what thoughts are chosen, not control what is chosen. The final choice is always up to the individual doing the choosing.

Situation: Your boss thinks you are not doing your best work. He says that he is very disappointed in you.

A thought for your files (*choose one*)

DEFECTIVE THOUGHT

I'm devastated. I feel that I am responsible for him feeling so disappointed in me. I'm disgusted with myself.

EFFECTIVE THOUGHT

I appreciate that he feels disappointed in me. He is entitled to his opinion. Yet I know I have been doing my best. However, I don't and can't control what he chooses to think. I'm not really responsible for his thought-choices any more than he is responsible for mine. I will, however, use some sound influencing tactics that may give him a more favourable impression about me and about the quality of my work.

Motivation: intrinsic vs extrinsic

The effective thinker aims to move people into action through intrinsic motivation (as opposed to extrinsic motivation). With intrinsic motivation, one has a proprietary interest in a given project or the success of a company or an idea. There is a sense of ownership and pride if you are involved in the development of something. If something is foisted on you, extrinsic motivation, a forced motivation, ensues, eg 'Do it because I said you should do it.' Although both intrinsic and extrinsic motivation might get the job done, the intrinsically motivated worker emerges a self-starter, an initiator, a builder, who is proud and loyal to the cause under consideration.

In addition, intrinsic motivation lasts much longer than forced motivation. One can push people, but if instead you give people sufficient freedom to find their own way, they will be self-starters and make lasting contributions.

Situation: you want one of your staff to demonstrate more initiative.

A thought for your files (*choose one*)

DEFECTIVE THOUGHT

'Get going. We've got a big job to do. If you don't shape up, you'll soon be shipping out.'

EFFECTIVE THOUGHT

I'll influence, not control him or her. There are a dozen ways of influencing at my disposal: setting a good example, positive reinforcement, appreciation, giving plenty of room for trial and error, etc. I'll let him or her become involved in the project at its inception.

Effective thinkers set a good example. They create a nurturing environment in which workers can take creative initiatives. Because they genuinely respects their people, their people tend to respond in kind. Effective thinkers appreciate that they cannot totally guarantee that they will always get back all that they give. They do not **demand** respect. They simply stack the odds in their own favour by earning respect.

Effective thinker Kaye Vasky: 'No matter how convincing or articulate a case I present, there is never a guarantee that my ideas will be accepted by someone else. So I present my case as eloquently and as articulately as possible. But the rest is up to the other person.'

At work, think of yourself as successful, right now

Long before they were a CEO, a President, or a Director, they were convincing others that their ideas were worthwhile and profitable, not only to the person they happened to be speaking to at that moment, but also to the organisation that both of them worked for.

For example, they carry themselves as if they are very successful in a given area long before they actually are. They make good use of powerful ideas, offer empathic listening to others, speak in regulated tones and use concise writing to influence others effectively.

> **Situation**: you're required to meet with another division of your company at a conference scheduled for next week.

A thought for your files (*choose one*)

DEFECTIVE THOUGHT

First impressions aren't particularly important.

EFFECTIVE THOUGHT

First impressions are extremely powerful, much more powerful than they deserve to be.

Therefore, I will do what I can to make the best first impression that I can. That's to my advantage. All I need do is figure out what kind of impression in this situation will be in my best interest and then go about making it.

As mentioned before, initial impressions apparently have so much impact that most of the time spent subsequent to the first impression is used to either validate or disprove that initial image. This, of course, is quite unfair to those people who make first impressions that are not equal to what they really are. Effective thinkers, however, use first impressions to great advantage.

Most of us prefer to believe that, as wise and prudent individuals, we will not put too much weight on our first impressions of others, but contrary to what we might like to believe, first impressions imprint deeply into our subconscious, even when we try to keep that from happening. Even if we attempt to withhold our final judgement about an individual that we've just met, that final judgement will still be based on proving whether or not our initial impression was valid or not. Effective thinking managers, knowing this, have as their policy, to take the image that they project, seriously. They know that success will be easier for them to achieve later on, if they get off to a good early start.

Image at work – 'prefer,' don't 'need' to influence

Effective thinker Fran Morgan: 'I've found that after I've made a reasonably decent first impression, I can usually let my hair down, and then do things my way with a minimum of hassle. However, if I don't make a good first impression, then it takes me an enormous amount of time and effort to correct that bad start. Sometimes it takes forever to be forgiven for an early mistake, but mistakes made after I'm already well-thought-of are readily overlooked.'

James Edwards: 'If walking into a meeting with a big smile, a tie, and a three piece suit has a payoff, and it does in my business (banking), then I do it.'

According to some 'image in business' research in the USA, medium blue suits have maximum appeal to those in average socio-economic brackets, whereas navy blue suits have maximum appeal to those in upper brackets. Of course this all depends on the corporate culture, the type of business, and even the country in which business is being conducted. However, since it is indeed possible that the shade of one's suit might make a difference and since effective thinkers are pragmatic enough to want to have influence, they make a study of what has maximum positive influence. Then, if it makes sense for them to do so, they pause and choose those thoughts that allow them to do so. Many other people, less effective, and less professionally successful than effective thinkers might say, 'The hell with all that image stuff. I dress the way I want and if the world doesn't like it, fine. That's the world's loss, not mine.' Effective thinking managers readily compromise themselves regarding principles that have no special validity for them.

Don Heath: 'I have no interest in worrying about compromising my life, just because I compromise on the way I dress. I definitely realise that dress is quite superficial when you look at the larger picture. But I find it very easy to play the image game. It's because I appreciate the larger picture, that I never waste my time insisting that I dress to suit my personality instead of dressing to influence others as needed.'

Situation: an order from 'above': 'As of next week, sales staff will be required to wear shirts and ties for men and suits or skirts for women.'

A thought for your files (*choose one*)

EFFECTIVE THOUGHT

What I wear isn't really me, but I know that the way I dress influences others. I can easily wear a shirt and tie/skirt, if I choose to do so. And I choose to do so.

DEFECTIVE THOUGHT

Not me. I don't go in for veneer. I'm into total authenticity.

In keeping with other things we've discussed about effective thinkers, please note the following. They do not have a **need** to influence others. They influence as a matter of **preference**. They influence out of choice, not need.

As successful influencers, effective thinkers are excellent at reading body language. They are sensitive to what others might be thinking and feeling, but they are never so preoccupied with what others are thinking, that they allow others to spoil their day. By using an artful blend of small talk, self-disclosure, productive listening, risk taking and openness, they do whatever is necessary to effectively influence others. Sometimes they even give advice.

Coaching as a means of influence

Here are some guidelines for using effective thinking in order to coach others influentially.

Exercise

Effective coaching and advising procedures

1 Have the individual who is to receive your coaching (your advisee) describe his or her issue of concern as clearly as possible, in about 10 minutes. Help your advisee to explain the situation to you by using charts, role play, diagrams or any other explaining device or devices.

2 Help your advisee to figure out the following:

- Things that he/she can possibly change about the issue.

  (Note: One can always change his or her own attitude.)

- Things that he/she cannot possibly change.

  (Note: If something cannot be changed, you can help the advisee grieve for that fact by going through denial, bargaining, anger and depression. Finally arriving at a healthy level of acceptance.)

- In concert with your advisee, develop a **3-step action plan** (in writing, with a starting date.)

Starting Date:________________

1 ____

2 ____

3 ____

Influencing by listening

Effective thinkers often ask themselves, 'Should I be listening to this, or should I not be listening to this?', whereas less effective people often listen to everything indiscriminately. So they often listen to the wrong thing or the wrong person at the wrong time or place. Listening to the wrong person, the wrong parts of what was said, or even worse, listening when nothing worthwhile is being said, can be totally 'defective.' For example, 'defective thinker' Pete Byers swallowed wholesale the advice his colleagues at work gave him regarding his role in the company's new project. 'I've got to stop pushing the company to expand. My friends told me so,' Pete reminded himself. But Pete's 'friends' were wrong. The project ultimately proved very successful, but poor Pete had backed out of it prematurely. If he had listened to his own gut reaction, rather than the opinion of his 'friends' in this instance, he would have emerged a winner. With sufficient respect for his own feelings, his aggressive tactics would have had tremendous payoff, not only for him, but for his company as well.

Effective thinker Louise Burns practices 'power listening.' She sorts out those times when it makes sense to listen to others and when it doesn't. Laura trusts her own judgement considerably more than Pete Byers does. Consequently, when Laura was advised by her boss to avoid conflicts with the competition, she resisted. 'I believe my present directions still make sense,' she explained, putting her job on the line. As a successful listener, Laura was attuned to her own inner drum beat. She knew intuitively that what she felt made sense and, therefore, came out a winner more often than not. 'I tend always to give myself excellent advice. After all, I'm familiar with the case. I've been on this case for 42 years so far.'

Situation: your direct subordinate becomes emotional and distraught over a terrible argument she has just had with her colleague. She phones you late in the evening and pleads with you to change her office location. You listen.

A thought for your files (*choose one*)

DEFECTIVE THOUGHT

I listen only to the content of what she says. She's really upset. This is terrible. She should never call me at home, especially at this hour.

EFFECTIVE THOUGHT

I listen to both content and feelings. I can appreciate her being upset. She is clearly very upset just now. I can listen primarily to her feelings and not to the content of what she is saying at the moment. However, if she still wants her office changed, I might then address the content of what she says.

Effective thinkers listen according to the nature of the situation. They do not listen in the same way in all situations. When it pays to listen to the content, they do so. When it makes more sense to listen to feelings they do that, and when it's wise to tune out altogether, they do that too.

One tired and haggard psychiatrist ran into a very relaxed, healthy looking friend whom he knew 25 years previously. They had both gone to the same medical school and later studied psychiatry together. 'Well, hello Dr Martin,' the first psychiatrist said to his old friend. 'You look absolutely wonderful. No wrinkles at all. You look as if life has been extremely easy. Look at me: I'm a haggard wreck. My psychiatric practice is killing me. All these years, listening every day to all my patients' complaints and aggravations. Absolutely killing, but you, Dan, you look wonderful. Hasn't being a psychiatrist got to you? Hasn't listening to all your patients' problems drained you? What's your secret?'

The other psychiatrist, Dr Martin, replied with an easy smile, 'Who listens?' Of course, this is an exaggeration, but the point is clear. If paying attention is of no consequence, effective thinking managers will often take it upon themselves to tune out and thus preserve their inner selves.

Another psychiatrist put it this way: 'Sometimes intensive listening can harm others. For example, if someone is very boring and you listen to that person attentively, are you being honest? No. The very act of your attentive listening only serves to reinforce the boring behaviour. Sometimes it's more honest to yawn, right in front of such an individual. That way you give him the benefit of honest feedback.'

Situation: one of your staff members is reaching out to you for emotional help.

A thought for your files (*choose one*)

DEFECTIVE THOUGHT

I listen to everyone and everything with a critical ear.

EFFECTIVE THOUGHT

I listen differently to different people in various situations. I sometimes listen to feelings and at other times to the content and at other times just for pleasure. This time, it's listening to feelings.

Listening for content requires analytical skill. The effective thinking manager's sharp critical thinking ability allows him to avoid being taken in by form over substance. Effective thinking managers know that words often obfuscate rather than clarify, that many things are rarely just as they appear to be on the surface.

Listening requires a mindset of empathy, not critical analysis. Many business people have never been listened to at the deepest level. Some people have never been heard on their own terms in their entire life. Listening to *feelings* is probably more difficult to do than listening to the *content*. Effective thinkers focus on listening to feelings because that kind of listening helps them become closer to others.

In order to set about listening, one must put into practice genuine caring and also offer accurate empathy for the person who is sharing. Martin Buber, a renowned philosopher, describes an 'I-Thou' attitude that reflects genuine caring. With an 'I-Thou' attitude as opposed to an 'I-It' attitude, one totally appreciates that it is a human that is being listened to. An 'I-Thou' encounter is a very special event, where, from the perspective of eternity, two human beings encounter each other at a given moment in time. 'I-Thou' requires two individuals in their brief journey through time to genuinely care and appreciate each other as someone very special. 'I-Thou' encounters can be awesome when one is reminded that for a given instant two people journeying through time at a given moment become close, sharing common communication together. An 'I-Thou' encounter rises above ethnic differences, social position and all of the other relatively less important aspects that go with being simply a human being.

In order to have an 'I-Thou' encounter, you must, for the moment, completely appreciate the individuality of the person you are listening to. None of the usual posturing that goes on so often in business is necessary or productive during 'I-Thou' encounters.

The second ingredient that makes for deep listening is accurate empathy, with emphasis on the adjective *accurate*.

For example, assume that an employee attempts to share with you an upset regarding the fact that one of his/her children is very sick. If you have not suffered sufficiently in your own life, it can be extremely difficult for you to accurately empathise with that individual. All managers who happen to be effective thinkers have permitted themselves to experience some suffering, garnering plenty of experience with the pain and anguish that is part of life. Experiences with difficult emotions permit them to identify with, and accurately connect with, the feelings of other persons who are sharing their difficulties.

While it is obviously quite unnecessary to undergo brain surgery just because the person whom you want to help is going through such an operation, it is still possible to extrapolate from your own life experiences of suffering that are very similar to the feelings the person you are listening to is likely to be experiencing!

Effective thinkers never mistakenly use sympathy to replace empathy when they deeply listen. Sympathy means feeling *for*, while empathy means feeling with. While sympathy might be better than not caring at all about another person, accurate empathy, not sympathy, is what is really needed. The sympathetic executive says, 'John, I feel sorry for you, what a shame.' The empathetic manager says, 'John, I can come close to appreciating you. I'm not you, but at the very least I can come close to experiencing just what you are feeling right now.'

John, upon receiving 'I-Thou' respect plus accurate empathy from the listener, will tend to feel appreciated, cared for, and helped, whereas with only sympathy, a somewhat holier-than-thou attitude is conveyed. 'Poor you' is not nearly as effective a type of listening as an 'I-Thou,' accurate empathy type of listening.

Situation: one of your staff complains privately to you about the boss and calls her an uncomplimentary name.

A thought for your files (*choose one*)

DEFECTIVE THOUGHT

I love hearing this: tell me more about the idiot (OR) stop, please: you can't speak disloyally about the boss this way.

EFFECTIVE THOUGHT

This person is simply sharing feelings with me. I'll listen to the feelings experienced and bear in mind that the issue is form, rather than substance. It's sometimes healthy to let a person bitch, if they do so with discretion.

Try, on occasion to create tension deliberately in business encounters. Consider standing up and leaving when another person is speaking excessively. Experiment with deliberately misunderstanding the content or the feelings of what a speaker shares, if it makes sense to do so. Consider slightly distorting what a speaker has said, deliberately putting words in the speaker's mouth. These tactics, of course, are only used to disconcert. Effective thinkers use defensive ploys of this type only on those rare occasions when a good offence serves as the best defence.

Tune in, tune out

Although effective thinkers attend and usually lead numerous meetings, they never suffer at boring meetings. At such meetings, effective thinking managers listen only to what is appropriate. Effective thinking managers are masters of tuning in and tuning out as needed: if a child is disruptive, or a spouse nags, they pay attention to find the reasons, but at the same time they tune out the 'noise.' If there is serious business at a meeting, he tunes in. If a secretary complains without justification, they again tried to find the real reasons, but tune out the excessive static.

However, no one would ever know any of this if they depended on the effective thinker's facial expressions or body language. They really know how to hide his/her inner feelings, whenever it makes sense to do so.'

Once I had a professor who was not entirely joking when he said, 'If you want to get your Ph.D, the trick is to take a seat in the front row, look the professor in the eye periodically, nod affirmatively, and say 'How true, how true.'

Effective thinkers who happen to be managers conserve their limited energies by listening only when it really makes sense to listen. While productive listening was considered much more important than speaking, according to effective thinking managers, they had similar ideas about speaking too. Effective thinking managers always weigh their words in business.

Effective thinkers speak when it makes sense to speak. At other times, they keep their opinions to themselves and they are very careful about anything that they put in writing. Some things are often better left unwritten. Although effective thinkers often keep private notes for themselves, they usually keep corporate memo writing to a bare minimum but when they do write, they see that what they write is properly written, checking for spelling and content very carefully.

In conclusion

Effective thinkers take the influence of others as something very important, but they realise that they never really control another human being. Consequently, they use listening, coaching, caring, presenting, negotiating and all other necessary skills required to be an excellent influence over others. They never fail to see life as very serious, but the business of influencing and managing as a game – a game to be played, win/win.

Influencing exercises

Drawing on what you know about influence, what effective thoughts apply to the following situations?

- You have a compelling urge to speak out strongly at a company meeting regarding certain controversial issues.
- You are 'required' to attend a party at the boss's home in honour of a colleague you've long disliked.
- You are nervous about giving a talk to the executive staff. Your entire future depends on how well you make this presentation.

PART THREE

SUMMARY

You have been given all **four** programmes to unlock the **two doors** to enormous **1** personal and **2** professional success.

Programme 1: Relentlessly aim to have a full and satisfying life.

Programme 2: Proactively choose thoughts that provide you with a full and satisfying life, but not at the expense of others.

Programme 3: Periodically assess your interpersonal strengths and weaknesses.

Programme 4: Systematically improve bit by bit.

Everything that we've covered in this book boils down to following two points:

Point 1

Get your mind to work for you through proactive effective thought choosing.

Point 2

Interrelating successfully with others will follow automatically.

EIGHTEEN
Sustaining your success

Since you presumably have read this far, you are well informed about being an effective thinker and, as an effective thinker, I am sure you fully appreciate the necessity of successfully getting your mind to work for you, before trying to interrelate well with others. Let's review all that we have covered.

- You appreciate why it is necessary to relentlessly aim to have a 'full and satisfying life.'
- You fully understand the meaning of 'full and satisfying.'
- You have made a lasting commitment to have a full and satisfying life, but not at the expense of any other person and you are making it your business to proactively choose thoughts that provide you with that kind of life.
- You know how your mind works and the connections between thoughts, feelings and behaviour.
- You have started to build an effective thought file of your own.
- You know how to create, when necessary, a battery of sometimes uncomplicated (but always very effective) thoughts, available to be chosen by you, whenever it makes sense to do so.
- You now fully appreciate the power of proactive thought choosing and you are now producing a great life (show) for yourself as the programme director of your own, wonderful Bodymind Theatre.
- You know how to pause. When you pause you know how to find and choose thoughts that are effective for the situation you face.

- You know how to support your thought choosing activity with subconscious strategies such as 90-second self-hypnosis, whenever it makes sense to do so.
- In addition, you have accessed your hidden identity, an inner identity that has elements of inner calm, passionate purpose with fun and adventure structured within it. You use this identity only as needed.
- On top of all this, you know how to use effective thinking to manage your ongoing and very important emotional life. Remember, your thoughts are the key to your existence, but your feelings (taking place under your own skin) is the place where you really live.
- With the elements of self-management clearly mastered, you are ready to successfully interrelate (actually, influence) others.
- You have taken an inventory of your interpersonal strengths and weaknesses.
- You have received or are going to soon receive, objective feedback to find out the effect that your persona has on others, especially those that you are in close contact with.
- You have been, and are going to, concentrate even more on systematically improving your shortcomings, bit by bit: continuous personal improvement.
- You know how, if you so desire, to become more effectively assertive, or how to become a more effective risk taker, or a more effective negotiator.
- You know how to be more effectively intimate if you want to be that way.
- You know how to be a better presenter if you want to be one.
- You have a firm grasp on how to be more effectively influential – for example in the practice of the professional management.
- You have a wide variety of tricks, tips and techniques at your disposal and if you need more, you know how to find or create them.

After all, you are an effective thinker and you appreciate that the main technique in dealing well with others is you as a whole person – a nurturing person with 'green fingers' for helping others to grow. **You are a person who clearly knows how to get your mind to work for you, before trying to interrelate with others**.

Appendix

The Mind Laundry Test Programme: the effective thinking self assessment

The following test will serve as a periodic review of the book that you have just completed. Take this test now and take it again periodically in order to sustain your success. This test will sensitise you to areas you may have been neglecting. Turn to the sections of the book that deal with those particular areas. Remind yourself of what it is that you have been neglecting and you will most certainly sustain your gains.

Directions: Please circle the number that indicates your level of agreement with each statement. Easy scoring instructions are at the end of the instrument.

1 I quickly turn most 'problems' that come my way into 'manageable projects.'

9	8	7	6	5	4	3	2	1
Agree								Disagree

2 I am a healthy sceptic, but definitely not a cynic.

9	8	7	6	5	4	3	2	1
Agree								Disagree

3 I have a clear inner identity, that goes far beyond my given name, my job title or even my family roles. I definitely know who I am – especially at the inner self level.

9 8 7 6 5 4 3 2 1

Agree Disagree

4 I have made the distinction between being reasonable and being realistic and I tend to be realistic more often than not.

9 8 7 6 5 4 3 2 1

Agree Disagree

5 I appreciate that anger stems from fear. Since I generally have very little to fear, I rarely get angry.

9 8 7 6 5 4 3 2 1

Agree Disagree

6 I consider myself a 'thought-chooser.' I practice pro-active thought choosing as much as it makes sense. I refuse to be an indiscriminate user or victim of any thought or series of thoughts that happen to 'come to mind.' I use every means I know of to help me take charge of whatever it is that I think.

9 8 7 6 5 4 3 2 1

Agree Disagree

7 No matter what my present state of mind, I still reserve the right to think that somehow, some way 'the best is yet to come.'

9 8 7 6 5 4 3 2 1

Agree Disagree

8 I appreciate that success is a journey rather than a destination and I make it my business to enjoy the journey as much as is humanly possible, but not at the expense of others.

9	8	7	6	5	4	3	2	1
Agree								Disagree

9 I understand and appreciate the value of listening to feelings and I do, when appropriate.

9	8	7	6	5	4	3	2	1
Agree								Disagree

10 When appropriate, I make good use of rapid self-hypnosis to assist me in effective thought choosing.

9	8	7	6	5	4	3	2	1
Agree								Disagree

11 I appreciate that values are caught rather than taught and try, therefore, to lead others by example.

9	8	7	6	5	4	3	2	1
Agree								Disagree

12 I fully appreciate that life is much too serious not to have a sense of humour about it and I do have a sense of humour about life.

9	8	7	6	5	4	3	2	1
Agree								Disagree

13 I am assertive when it makes sense to be assertive.

9 8 7 6 5 4 3 2 1

Agree Disagree

14 I tend to turn so-called 'failures' into positive 'learning experiences.'

9 8 7 6 5 4 3 2 1

Agree Disagree

15 I tend to have 'preferences,' rather than absolute 'needs.'

9 8 7 6 5 4 3 2 1

Agree Disagree

16 When it comes to dealing with, I realise that that takes place only by 'influence' and not by control of others. I realise that the only thing I fully control is my own thought choices, not the thought choices of others.

9 8 7 6 5 4 3 2 1

Agree Disagree

17 When making a presentation I know how to manage myself first, then my material and then the audience.

9 8 7 6 5 4 3 2 1

Agree Disagree

18 I negotiate to win/win as much as possible.

9 8 7 6 5 4 3 2 1

Agree Disagree

19 I appreciate the value of coaching and know the steps involved to coach effectively.

9	8	7	6	5	4	3	2	1
Agree								Disagree

20 I know how to get close to people that are very important to me. I know when and how to trust others and myself.

9	8	7	6	5	4	3	2	1
Agree								Disagree

21 I leave myself open for constructive criticisms from time to time. I make objective periodic self-assessments that relate to managing others. I have an action plan for improving my weaknesses.

9	8	7	6	5	4	3	2	1
Agree								Disagree

22 I know how to manage my emotions and do so, when appropriate.

9	8	7	6	5	4	3	2	1
Agree								Disagree

23 I am an effective risk taker. I take wise, not indiscriminate, risks, but I do take risks.

9	8	7	6	5	4	3	2	1
Agree								Disagree

24 I appreciate that, in general, people tend to treat you the way that you teach them to treat you. I teach people to treat me with respect.

9	8	7	6	5	4	3	2	1
Agree								Disagree

25 I appreciate that business is a game and that life is serious and I play 'the management game' to win.

9	8	7	6	5	4	3	2	1
Agree								Disagree

26 I value quality over quantity, in relationships, in the things I do and in life.

9	8	7	6	5	4	3	2	1
Agree								Disagree

27 I face the harsh realities of life directly, grieve rapidly for them when appropriate, then get on with my life, living it as effectively as possible, from that point on.

9	8	7	6	5	4	3	2	1
Agree								Disagree

Scoring: total all of the numbers that you have encircled.

If your total was between 252 and 224, you are, indeed an effective thinker and have the tools for being a top manager in your field.

If you scored between 223 and 112, you are currently in the middle range. You can expect to become, in a relatively short time, highly successful with your own mind and in dealing with others, but be careful, because a person in your position can go either way – either up or down. Take time, now, to review your various responses to each item on this self assessment, and re-read those sections that apply to those items where you scored 6 or less.

Finally, if you scored 111 or less, you are in the lowest third. You undoubtedly are more than a bit self-defeating, especially when it comes to job satisfaction or personal life satisfaction. Re-read the sections of this book that apply. When you are able to score high on this test, on every item – you will be fully prepared to successfully get to understand how your mind can work *for* you to the benefit of *both* yourself and your dealings with others. Just remember, you can be successful through effective thinking. And remember, regardless of your score – the best is yet to come!

NOTES

NOTES